Psalms of Anarchy

Psalms of Anarchy

Angelo Jaramillo

Ally,

... for what never might've
been, and all that we
never could've imagined.
May God and his disciples
forever envy our own
insignificance.

Peace To The War machine
that Controls Everything.

with
love,

SUNSTONE
PRESS

SANTA FE

Sunstone books may be purchased for educational, business, or sales promotional use.
For information please write: Special Markets Department, Sunstone Press,
P.O. Box 2321, Santa Fe, New Mexico 87504-2321.

Library of Congress Cataloging-in-Publication Data

Jaramillo, Angelo, 1976-
  Psalms of anarchy : poems / Angelo Jaramillo.
    p. cm.
  ISBN 978-0-86534-625-3 (pbk. : alk. paper)
  I. Title.

PS3610.A73P77 2007
811'.6--dc22

                          2007045242

WWW.SUNSTONEPRESS.COM
SUNSTONE PRESS / POST OFFICE BOX 2321 / SANTA FE, NM 87504-2321 /USA
(505) 988-4418 / ORDERS ONLY (800) 243-5644 / FAX (505) 988-1025

Dedicated to my Father,
Thomás Miguel Benedicto Jaramillo
For Everything.
I Love You.

Contents

Preface / 11

**Book I / 13
Depression**

I Feel Like An Animal / 15
Don't Ever Call Me A Fuckin Poet / 16
An Existential Movement / 17
Humanity Is A Sickness / 18
Desperation I / 19
Walking On Sidewalks / 20
First Life of Labor / 22
The Swamp / 23
I Hate The Fuckin Wind In Las Vegas / 25
Redemption / 26
The Dismal Future / 27
Death Is A Tattoo / 29
Desperation II / 30
Heretical / 31
Desperation III / 38
Recuperation Is Impossible / 39
III / 40
Gyrus / 41
Anti-Father's Day / 42
Sometimes I Masturbate Four Times In One Day / 45
Inevitable Lust / 46
Caged Animal Love / 47
The Epitome of Stupidity / 51
Love Your Oppressor / 52
Hate Those That Hate You / 53
Troublemaker / 54

Killer of Religion / 55

The System 57

No More Birthdays / 59

On A Trip / 64

Pussy In Your Mouth / 67

August 30, 2000 3:27pm / 68

Desperation IV / 72

Book II / 73
Lamentation

Soulless Woman / 75

Some Corny Ass Shit to Say to a Lonely Older Woman
As She's Crying Over Her Failing Second Marriage / 76

Portrait of a Woman / 77

I Know a Womyn / 78

Accidental Moments / 82

Listening To Tom Waits In Psychiatric Ward Gloom / 84

Tribute / 88

A Makeshift Dream / 90

Zoë / 93

Pilgrimage / 95

Slavocracy / 96

Shadow of Tomorrow / 98

Enigma / 99

Process of Creation / 100

Dire Inhalation / 101

Spiritual Displacement / 102

Lynx-Eyed / 103

To My Mother & Father / 105

Timelessness / 106

The Meaning of Holiness / 108

Heaven By Default / 110

Some People / 113

Yes / 114

Blake / 116

The Perils of Abstinence / 117

Strange Karma / 118

Juniper Eyes / 120

The Fortunate Misfit Who Counts Blessings / 125

Ephemeral / 126

Skeletal Remains / 127

Nameless / 128

Calm / 130

Something Beautiful / 132

The Requiem / 133

The Beautiful Distraction / 135

Dear Anonymous / 139

Nothing / 141

The Valentine / 143

Book III / 149
Emancipation

...And The Pursuit of Happiness / 151

In The Workplace / 152

Utilitarian Reassurance of Personality in Capitalist Society / 153

Southpaw Go Home / 154

Insubordination / 157

Killer Cop, Killer Cop, Don't Stop! / 158

The Dirty Sanchez / 162

Ode to Phudds / 164

Job / 165

The Crosshairs / 167

Strip Joint Politics / 170

The Progressive / 172

Pledge of Allegiance Revised / 173

The Resistance / 174

The Eleventh Commandment / 175

Aagghhhh! / 181

Land of Disenfranchisement / 192

My Beautiful Palestinian Brother / 199

The Day George Herbert Walker Bush Died / 212

The Broken Heart / 226

*I'd rather live one day like a lion
than live one hundred years like a lamb.*

—Anonymous

Preface

This book is not about anarchy. This book is not about anarchy as perceived by those who think they know something about anarchy whether they are anarchists or not.

This is not a book of poetry. This is not a poetry book.

This is a book.

I write.

Many of the pieces in this book were written around the invasion of Iraq somewhere between March of 2003 and the time of publication of this book. Many of the words are of a severe political nature on purpose. For those who don't like to mix politics and art, I don't write for you.

For those who could care less...thank you.

As far as poetry is concerned, I am not a poet. I am not a writer. I am not an artist.

If you know how to read and you like to read, please read this text. If you think you are some kind of intellect because you graduated from college or you have a graduate degree or two or three or a Ph.D., or you are some sort of important professional who lives a life revolving around money, please read this book.

This book is not an example of how to write or what to publish. I do not want this book to sell a million copies. I want this book to reach the hands of millions preferably by hook or crook.

This is a book.

Book I
Depression

I Feel Like An Animal

I feel like an animal,
      subjected to the cruel
            wrath of nature—
                  no control over my
                      thoughts,
                            emotions,
                                  sensations,
                                          or being.

Don't Ever Call Me A Fuckin Poet

I wrote poetry,
escaping midnight
police chases…
      unfulfilled
is how I feel
when I viciously
stare into a jagged
mirror, reflecting
what I wasn't.

Can we trust our own reflections?

An Existential Movement

The man said "NO" in time to flee the Earth.
Blessed is him who dares the shares of mirth.

One's fight through inner light can kill all time.
Eternal sight starts singing frightful chime.

Despite the blissless fun without a drug,
Heaven prayed wrong, too late for my own hug.
So please let go before we lose all self,
I see the point beyond complacent wealth.

Jean-Paul once claimed, "I am, 'thou dost exist."
With God and Life and Love I too am pissed.

Humanity Is A Sickness

Humanity is a sickness,
wishing to be destroyed.
Unemployment rates keep rising,
summer winds sneeze toxic carbon-oxygen,
the super rich punish the poor with impunity.

There is no such thing as a livable community.

In the land of opportunity,
       death squads
       launch congressional laws
       to blockade the have-nots
       from having anything.

marginalization blinded

Desperation I

Haunted…
is there no escape from life
besides death?
            Depression
            is stillness.
Calm ambiance,
        no dance
can cure the delusional sickness
celebrating throughout my
vital carcass. Ubiquitous disease—
corroded mind wandering amongst
            manic nocturnal insomniacs,
                lamenting over
                the irreparable past
                never forgotten.
How rotten it is to exist
without freedom.
How sorrowful it would be
to see love and not rape her.
                I can't get over
                feeling sorry for my
                useless, worthless self.

but do we not rape
freedom when it is
given to us?

I loathe my own
propensity for self-pity

Walking on Sidewalks

Cracked destiny...
Concrete fragments of imaginary
friends. I pretend to care
to pretend to live.

As the protruding jutting weeds holler
to feed,
I squeeze blood from my
       scarred wrists.

The velocity of
The broken city atrocity remains
Stuck in a permanent state
Of incarcerated vertigo.

Nothing is sacred anymore
but misguided intuition
and brainwashed premonitions
of submissive masses.

Temples of worship are institutions of societal confusion.

Forgetfulness of regrets
      accumulating my guilty neurosis;
I stop to sniff
a snails slimy stomach—pepper sneezes,
           mountain valley breezes,
           the teasing doesn't stop
           after adulthood.

I don't need money on this
mundane quest for celestial
vision;

materialistic experts in mainstream materialism can't express precision.

We were told that our decisions don't
matter and yet the fast-food keeps
making me fatter and fatter and obese;
as vulnerable as charred geese served
on steaming Thanksgiving snobby platters.

Shattered reflections—
Catastrophic desire feeds the fire
of amoral behavior—
there doesn't seem to be a savior of any religion—
humankind continues to waste away
beneath the dungeon of static resurrection.

I walk on sidewalks
To talk to the dead ones that are
More alive than the swine
In line to destroy what
Was once mine…
survivors of these apocalyptic times.

First Life of Labor

Just contracted HIV,
     dick wasn't hard enough for safety,
        condoms tore
            what a sighing bore it is to live.

Fell asleep today,
     mid-summer breezes forgotten,
        the sleazebags the owners of property,
          the unaccounted lives shot.

Lectures of terrifying peace—
cardiograms required every month—
lepers look as beautiful as pink dawns
seen through serene smoke screens;
                feet sizzle
             blood trickles
          no time to waste except your own,
          not even a raw turkey bone could
          cure the amplified hound's woes.

So much for this and that,
So preoccupied with death,
                I saw my mother naked again,
                sing a song bereft.

The auditor at my closed door
knocks, pounds with heavy face;
happiness ended when
I became a permanent member
of the rat race.

The Swamp

I sold my soul for a copper Lincoln,
I killed my mother with love.
I fornicated with a Scottish terrier,
only to hear it was unheard of.
The Holy City has become unholy,
the mother Earth no longer shares.
The Planet Jupiter surrounds us all
waiting for Venus to undo her mahogany hair
...and still...
for seven hundred some years, lost in one second,
the land of Northern New Mexico has been auctioned off
to the low-life capitalist, conducted by a Ring of Santa Fe advocates
calling themselves Santa Fean, while another Santa Fesino
found himself locked out of the New San Francisco.
Cherished are the perishable items of an immigrant's home, *we pillage our*
imperialistic language, amalgamated heritage, *heritage*
my younger children know no rest throughout the winter's hermitage.
Radioactive industries must be redeemed
gleaming with governmental contracts that
make fat cats of any region employ religion
like Communist China cuddling Tibet…

you can't free anyone with a bumper sticker.

You sold your soul for a millimeter of wine,
You slaughtered your father with affection.
You forgot to use a condom with nonoxynol-9
when you fucked your fuzzy palm without an erection
...and yet...
Brigadier-General Stephen Watts Kearney stampeded in here in 1846,
just to make us sick with his crooked Amerikan agenda;

today we worship you with your
blood, bleach, and brine—demagogic propaganda;
because you teach us not to think for ourselves,
because our brain is washed with soaked cloths
of digital satellite dishes fulfilling unfulfilled wishes
of colorful magazines expressing sexual bigotry
constantly, forever reducing our creative potential
to instrumental macro-machinations cowering
behind cubby holes where silence is an explosion
of repressed submission.

*may I not
allow myself
to be imitated*

I Hate the Fucking Wind in Las Vegas

I hate the fucking wind in Las Vegas!

We were introduced when my ride broke down.

As the dust devils and runaway trash

become additional victims to the

wrath of nature's reckless whistling grievance,

stinging breezes slap my fresh countenance,

micro particles swim inside these eyes,

traffic lights tremble and tree tops twist up

the echoes heard from the whole universe;

I begin to climb the atmosphere.

Redemption

What the fuck am I going to do now that I am dead? I suppose I shall just go on living like I always did. Before I embark on my dark journey, I will first take a glance at the dance known as my burial ceremony. Plenty of phonies and cronies pray to the designated giver of life to show some sort of clemency on such a soul that was alone, but never lonely. Funny how funerals, like weddings, are only farce produced so money can take all the credit. Regret it? Regret what, how I chose to pose as a happy figure whom of life I was bigger? The womb is the tomb that ultimately numbs my pnuema. These heretics, spics, associates, and pricks tend to condescend my memory by sobbing for no reason. It is devastating treason to genuine hypocrisy! My philosophy was only ridiculed and patronized like uneven eyes on small guys. What a hypnotic sham. Goddamn those foes of mine who never gave time to a miser who was wiser than destiny. They now hold bright flighty flowers near their breast to suggest some kind of recompense for evolving decadence. Sure, go ahead, bow your heads in solemn rows of brown glossy benches, you sons of bitches, snitches, and dirty thirty-year old wenches who wear veils in order to mask your masks. Ask for my forgiveness once more to define the score that was never uneven, just broken. Every tear you drop is a slap on my cheek. Every blessing bestowed is a defeat for the meek. Hush this nonsense before I blush and discover a purposeful destination. Hug one another to smother the one you never offered your brother. Only my mother and father are sincere for the rest are too near fear to see through me like a seer. How queer? Don't get me wrong, all your sad songs resonate like a gong or a bong but next time try not to wait too long or the gate to bliss will be the only thing missed. All I request is that you forget and detest the best encounter you ever had, just to remain in pain eternally mad for failing my test as I prevail as the purest manifest jest who is now given the honor of everlasting rest.

The Dismal Future

Escape the dismal future,
doing push-ups on a bra…

Fela Kuti's bare bone alto sax, dime bags, and greasy fingertips covering
the reflection of a melancholy fever; this folly of filth is not worth the
birth of Christ.
Subjugated like a 19th century renegade slave searching
for freedom in a stolen land. The devil's hideaway revels
in the misery of those infected with hope;

dope is the only passage of time.

Broken marriages, disparages of carriages rocked off the treetop.
Burnt to the gravel by nuclear disasters—
mistakes of forsaken humanity.

iT iS cYCLICAL iNSANITY tHAT pERMEATES oUR tHOUGHTS!

Dear President, Dear Pope, Dear Prime Minister, Dear Chancellor of
Chaos:
Anarchy is the solution to communists as communism is the solution
to capitalists as capitalism is the solution to Judaism as Judaism is the
solution to Islam as a Muslim fucks a Christian fucking the Tsotsi fucking
Santeria practiced by the religiosity of faggots.

The world is sick,
dying of a cancer gnawing at the outer left jaw of Bob Marley
puffing on a coma stick.

People are fake, ugly, rotten, misbegotten like
Eugene O'Neil writing a play for elitists.
One more award show on the televisitation programmer
is needed to convince monkeys they are a greater species
than pigs pretending to be human.

Suicide is not a solution Ozzy...
Euthanasia is.

Death Is A Tattoo

When death occurs, life cries. The eyes may claim to be the portal to the soul, but the soul travels incognito. The soul cries for itself. We live with death. Contrary to people's stupid opinions, people don't have free will. The will of the people has never been free. Only death can provide freedom. Freedom is not Faith Hill singing on some cellular phone advertisement, earning spare change for a Negro who is incapable of earning it for himself, by himself, with himself. Freedom is Faith Hill giving the Negro a blowjob, then the Negro giving her the money. Freedom is death in the sense that no one lives. Life is not to be lived, but to take advantage of. The ace in the hole is the queen of spades—God—the self-inflicted creator. God must've been melancholy for eternities when God created these things called us. The price to pay for freedom is death and the price to pay for death is life and the price to pay for life is your soul. We are not the butterfly, we are the vulture. We are not the koala, we are the termite. Extinct is how we exist. Extinct to a soul and a ubiquitous fiend that decided to put us here. Science says we're an accident. Either way I feel like an abortion. We maneuver through decomposing willow trees sprouting poisonous mushrooms to make us high, to allow us to die. Imagine if we never died. How could we have a concept of life? Only if we consume death can we control it. Death is a bribe. Death is a tattoo. God is a whore and his or her creations are worthless. Humans cannot be the pinnacle of all existence.

Desperation II

I hate this fuckin world.
I hate this fuckin life.
I will never smell the sinewy cunt
      of my future wife
         undergoing rigor mortis.
Her lunatic clitoris,
vigilant intaglio
preceding xenia.

Heretical

I'm obsessed with death
like a horny Lucifer stoically staring at the human race, above the
    bottom layer crust of the Earth. Living life is too expensive, not worth
    the unilateral purchase buying into mega-consumerism. Each day,
    next day...
an avant-garde wave of digital surfers create the silent harmony;
peace escapes from a prison cell made of lice, licking the salt-ridden
    wounds
of a very similar convict doing a stank impression of Steve McQueen
    breathing.
Inside drug-induced memories and wax-smitten smiles, feigning the
    appreciation of attaining a still better life bequeathed by a higher
    standard of not living, friendship falls apart like the Berlin Wall
    copulating with a nervous sledgehammer.

Freedom is not being allowed to live a life not wanted.
Freedom is bathing in a three-legged rusty bathtub without water.
Against nature, against creation, I dramatize suicide by not committing a
    sin.

A sleepless spirit carefully meanders through the polluted puddle of
    curdled milk in the mixed cocktail of a galaxy—somewhere there
    is a reverberation of degrading fantasies singing our names in
    unison. Zero blessings given to a featherless parakeet using a plastic
    microphone without a chord, without an inaudible loudspeaker,
    listening to scratched compact discs, listening to warbled tape
    recorders, listening to old voices jostling inflamed throats, screeching
    the blood letting tunes to a spring concentration camp concentrated
    in a never-ending race of rats wasting.
The demon underneath will die by living, by seeking, by dreaming,
demanding another chance to do what she shall never do, what she
    never did.

Sleep my infected child…expose the crippled man lying
motionless under a glass bed in the morning before the yawning dawn;
yank the bleeding sun from its gallows, you shall fall on top the
    decomposing carcass of a salivating German Shepard with no legs,
    dragging itself on a concrete dirt road by its decaying incisors—
    hunting without hope.

Twisted spiral after vertical spiral after DNA replica, did the depressed
    scientists forget that we still live in a world we can still sense?

I see all forms of creatures dying of famine, disease, and loneliness.

I was born stillborn.

Look at the baby grasshopper whispering to the leper about the
    morning dew, discussing the bogus ramblings of diabetic politicians
    making love to a defibrillator unplugged.
Musings become more sedated as father time becomes another.
    Mothers
and daughters and nuns and devil-worshipping priests sing Hebrew
    hymns of hypnotic gestures.

The gouged-out eyelids of a Harvard professor would compensate for
    the prune skin of the immortal Samuel Beckett. An invisible splash of
    bacterial water foments atop the bald summit of Socrates' ecstasy!

I don't feel like reading. I don't feel like writing. I feel like eating a
    fertilized angel hair cake, sucking it trough a torn straw, and licking
    the slimy internals of a cricket.

Mesmerized by increasing levels of benign radiation—
Tormented by boxcars without wheels, running downhill—
Fascinated by naked women with feminist ideologies—
Compromised by holy lottery tickets already expunged in a
toilet bowl filled with spongy bowels tasting like cataracts.

Did the settled blazing saddle of a sun swallow you like Jonah
    swimming in a tub?
Black widows spin silky portraits of pubic hairs shrinking from the light.
Inspiration is unsound, threatened with extinction like a Bengal tiger
    traced by
Henri Rousseau with a colorless crayon…

Simpletons are Gods.

Place an emerald magnifying glass on your tongue for two hours and
    absorb the diving sunrays hiding behind a paper curtain of fog. No
    one can see but a yellow smiley face on a black T-shirt wearing
    a frown; no one can believe unless one lies to oneself about the
    birth of the present moment, the death of the first day of Earth, the
    birth of a totem-pole with six eyeless masks—a playwriting beggar
    mounting the skins of dead fur with its scarred forehead; a Japanese
    samurai praying to a Chinese Goddess about Jesus like tulip petals
    playing billiards inside a cardboard box; a voodoo doll with a
    crimson painted skull; tragedy and comedy reciting the entire bible
    of black arts in semi-reverse; Frida Kahlo plucking her eyebrow with
    silk toothpicks, placing each individual hair in the ear of a butchered
    snow fox; and Rodney King displaying an unforgivable smile with no
    teeth—the yearnings of the dead in denial.

Near-sighted, autistic gifted, neurotic, worshipped as the melting
    golden calf, frightened of the semblance of a shadow that poses as
    unrecognizable reflection; broken mirrors equal seven years invested
    in seven sinister acts of sarcasm. Shivering every morning, I attempt
    to brush teeth. The sticky top of the tube lived beneath a brownish
    cap, fingers reeked. The gel climbing out of the tube sock fingered
    my stinging crowns with its bitter texture and disarming taste. Black
    licorice smells like burning hair sprayed with Drakkar cologne.
    Congested water swims through the miniature sewer tunnel; the
    reddish purple ooze hasn't ceased to drip on my tongue. How erotic
    the trivial persuasions that tease my oral testicles.

Something about her feet that make me swivel to jazz in a wooden seat.

I hear a midnight confession. It is the enormous voice in my head
  giving me a baptismal sermon on the goodness of spirit. Miraculous
  disbeliefs, paganism, and nihilistic speeches reap the sowing of my
  vanity. I am necrophilia holding hands with dead children under the
  age of eight, singing an in-of-tune version of Crimson & Clover.

  Pass me a contagious needle,
  my last days are too far away,
  sour milk from wrinkled breasts
  makes the world stand still; death
  said I would be saved by a man wearing
  sandals made of hemp. The soothsayers
  warn us of the reigning doomsday that is already
  present, here, today, now, this momentary
  ridicule that are lies worshiped by God.

I am incapable of learning who or what I am.
The Earth is not worth saving because we keep procreation
a cycle of sickness. Forsake us some more, scorch us with a **vibrating**
locomotive and prick our ears for blisters leaking blue piss.
Veins are weak. The clawing of demons climbing out
of Gehena—the itching of dry skin.
In the place of myself I have replaced a
displaced mask left behind in an African heist of original birth.

I am the abortion.

The vestiges of virginal wombs calm the avalanches of sandy desert hills.
I slide and slide and slide and slide and slide and slip.
Remove my gall bladder, it has turned white...
Slice my eyelids, they protect me from tears...
Tickle my belly button with a falcon's feather...
kill me. kiss me. keep me. kick me. kidnap me. kowtow me. kindle
me.
Give me kindness.

I am as relentless as gentleness.

The barren region of the Brazilian Amazon is home to
indigenous insects that have been infected by Western Civilization.
The world no longer cares about frightened laments of vociferous
mutilations. The anomalistic dictator covered in mucus
maneuvering particles of democracy, laughing like a hypocritical
hyena. The pain, the clutches for the surface of breath have left me
in a paper wheelchair, parading the twinkling halls like a war veteran
peddling a soapbox derby uphill, sporting a Moroccan velvet hat,
dangling a black tassel made of brown tinsel. Outside the burnt
tribal village, chinches of pastel colors gnaw at my bone marrow.
Bogart stares at me with sleep starved eyes, bloodshot as freshly
burned bullet holes and sombre owl feathers. Alaskan dead whales
make excellent dog food.

What a bitch that I was born.
Selfish as an Amerikan white male.
The prototype,
Xeroxed type of cloned human beings
that we are. Don't admit the devil is in you,
peeking through a wooden closet like that punk in Blue Velvet,
wetting his pants with a sore penis, too many orgasms in one
hour make you feel sick, like being horny for too long.
One more cold sore inside my mouth will varnish my tongue.
I'm dying like eighty-year olds. The only cancer I covet is life.
Inside my brain there lives a fortunate hobo:
tastes like a blind spider.

The tingling inside my cranium mechanism makes
me feel soft like a one-year old tomcat in heat.

Paradise is in my pocket.
Meal tickets were given to Catholics and Jews
when Hitler became the most revered demi-god sitting on a
broken toilet...the incinerator is home.
Earth has been forgotten like a one nightstand.

Earth is a one-night stand providing awkward cunnilingus.
Find me underground obnoxiously sipping tea with moles and
centipedes cut into three and a half segments…positively:
Picturing the glass is half-full is reversing the effects of global warming.
Positive thinking is destroying our world. If one thinks positive and in
positive textures, then negative volitions run out of extremity before
the fire consumes every arthritic senior citizen within torture chambers
made of cisterns. Sunken purple brown eyes stare outside smeared
windows to pinch a touch of vanishing sunshine.

A forgotten minority
of hypocritical thinking.

Writing on the graffiti ridden bed wall, spelled with voodoo curses of
reverse numerical satanic blessings. Nobody wants to listen to you if you
have something to say. They want their Super Bowl Sunday in a
plastic bag, supplemented with wine already contaminated with
Hepatitis C saliva,
spittle that is elixir of my suffering for nothing.

Fuck all the Gods of human documented history!

I am not free.

I dance as a lunatic on dextroamphetamines,
taking off his clothes
in front of familial relatives that are hustlers of a counterfeit breed;
the Oedipal Complex of conflict with the Amerikan Dreamer.
MBNA Amerika has just raised my credit limit to $3500 when I have a
debt of $2953.46, and a budget like the Amerikan Government; spent
for the rich and not the poor. Someone needs to take a suicide bomb
mission straight to Carnegie Hall and Rockefeller Center.

I have just now separated from everybody.

I am an anarchist member of the restless many.

I listen to Rage Against the Machine with sincerity.
With a love that is dead.

I wish I was dead.

Desperation III

Debussy's gentle spirit meditatively swims
through chipped ivory channels of delicate
piano keys,
gruesome melodies were not
created for the mentally ill.
We all become insane by the desperate age of twenty;
waffling adolescence taught us nothing.
There is no cure for anything.
Endure a lifetime of suffering with pleasure,
treasure immeasurable measure of uncontrollable
nervousness.
Paranoia is a constant companion
calmly chanting paralyzed lullabies,
neurotically waving good-bye
as detonated sleep steals
second base of a trampled sand diamond.
Stomach coughs,
sickly wheezes,
clumsily sneezes
the remaining
grayish blood and red
viscid slippery secretion
childishly jabbing for hierarchical
privilege
upwards on out
my deteriorating
scab-ridden
esophagus.

Recuperation is Impossible

Mistakes are made
frequently.
Thumb-printed torn
baseball cards are
traded for a fix.
        Will this torture of
        existence never subside?
        Must I continue to
        pay full price for a
        free ride of life unwanted?
I feel so sick I could vomit riddles,
  feel so sad I could torment puddles
  of hazy reflections.

        So much for success when the best of the worst are the best of
           what's left.

A G-cleft sings the blues
only for fools submitting
to covetous distractions.

        Inaction is satisfaction building phony flimsy concoctions of
           forgiveness.

There's not a human on Earth
that has achieved a sustainable
position of spiteful mirth.

Shaven centaurs shoot flaccid arrows
to erase my looted past.

Life is demeaning.

III

Remember nothing that is worth remembering.

I'm spiritually dismembered,
discombobulated like a rubber super ball ricocheting off
shattered mirrors and broken promises.

Does my creator love me?

I'm so deliberately blasphemous that
I will never prosper in the afterlife.

Who here who thinks knows that what we call life feels more like death?

I'm still waiting to be born.
I'm torn like Natalie Imbruglia's shiny soaked one time wonder pop star
     pussy
after she slept with Lenny Kravitz's first sell-out guitar.

Every time I have sex I panic.

How many angels must be thrown out of heaven before my soul is
     redeemed?

Gyrus

The days pass on...I'm not sure whether I'm alive or dead. There is no immediate concept of time in my tiny disinherited universe. Sometimes I feel I'm too alone and not willing to encounter others as disgusting. What is this sensation that fills up my violated bosom? This tingling, riveting around my stretched nerves and wrinkled bones; I keep having strong memories of moments that I thought disappeared long ago; simultaneously experiencing the terrible presence of déjà vu more than ever. Something is happening to me, I haven't a sarcastic notion what it is or could be. Mature enough to laugh at existence. Nothing to do but cry internally. Everything seems hopeless. I think I'm sick, like a schizophrenic hypochondriac. My body is speaking to me. Ignorance isn't not knowing; it is consciously choosing to dismiss what you are already aware of. I'm aware the stars at night are not as bright as they used to be. I'm fully aware that the world is ending. I once thought my life was only beginning. Where is salvation hiding? Where is redemption lurking? All of us must have redemption at the conclusion of our profane reality.

Anti-Father's Day
in memory of Mother's Day

Ceremony is for shit.
Quit thinking I might appreciate
the truth that does not exist.

God did not give hostile birth to you nor I,
so why debate it any longer? No longer are the bothers
and worries such as hungry kittens and starving babies.
Motherhood and fatherhood are crooked, blessed sounds
of nothing to be found but a broken promise
toppled with forgotten and forgiving tears.

I smear your White bred surname
that turned history into a broad board game.
Shame to the same that claimed the Earth as its owner.
Sooner not later, later and sooner, later is how the alligator
ate the moon with a sprinkle of sparkle beneath a
dazzling ballerina wearing second-hand make-up.

Feel the morning worship of dawn trying
to greet us with a kiss from Grace,
the wet dream of this jerk.
Even Steve Martin isn't as perverted
as a Christian upbringing.

Your mother I never loved, just coveted with prayer.

It didn't affect me when you told me you weren't married.
Somehow at some inconsequential moment in this pathetic life you
    didn't have to bring into this vomit, I almost realized we weren't
as connected as I never really quite hoped.

My Norteno redneck hillbilly father lives in an Eisenhower recurring dry
    dream,
my mother brainwashed me into believing the Left was here.
Marriage is for idiots.

      Our logic is tragic,
      black magic couldn't
      cure the woes of a
      hobo who isn't a homo,
      despite your misgiving
      beliefs.

My father sits in a bended knee-folding chair,
gazing towards hell with a remorseful smirk, similar
to McVeigh as he furtively squealed, "Farewell."
Jingling a wooden walking staff that crunches against
the molten cheeks of a junkyard dog taking a piss
on an immobile elevator outside,
he plots the underhanded undertaking of the good evils
that charmed his life like a used smudge stick...

Can it be that we will be no more?
Could it be that I trusted a pig that had rusted wings,
                      but didn't fly without the propellers
                      of the district attorney?
My family and your family are the amaranthine contagion evolving
throughout our life that never surely was a sizzling orgasm.
Squeeze my dilapidated hips, teeter tottering
to the dispassionate croons of Dean Martin and Pat Boone.

Lost and useless,
the blessed life of angels
tortured in the basement...
rotting away inside cesarean residue
of The Virgin's onomastic apology.

Drinking mephitic water from a boiling spring
sobbing in an untrammeled perverted mountain hill;
Our creator may not be benevolent,
our beloved frailties remain at a standstill.

Who knows who you are and who really gives a fuck.
In this short stint of a so-called world we run out of luck.
Your life failed twice throughout a haunted fiscal chapter
of the Amerikan Nightmare, now you're the one they're after.
One lady saved you, the one you call a bitch and an ominous curse.
But if you were living elderly, alone...could it be worse?
Of course, it's the rest of your unfulfilled existence that matters.
I refuse to spitefully excite you with politically rhetorical bullshit.
No one loves you more than the one you married not,
the one you hope isn't really your son,
but has a big nose, curly hair, is boisterously despondent, and wishes he
were no longer sooner rather than later...but only in a pseudo sense.

Father's only day is for shit and Mother's lonely day can suck my dick as
    well.
The only day that counts is the day in your life of breath and death,
everything in between is either God's or Satan's lighthearted spell.

Sometimes I Masturbate Four Times In One Day

Sometimes I masturbate four times
in one day.

Lessons aren't to learn,
the burning snow falls slowly.

What it is to be lonely
it is to live alone.

Outside my soul
the world is failing,
humanity is bailing out
of this sanctimonious morality play.

The sun doesn't shine on arbitrary holidays.

Some days,
        Sometimes,
                my childish rhymes make no sense.

Somewhere
        there is a lover for me
                inoculated against recompense.

The sound of syncopated beats
turns the soiled sheets of my
vacant bed blood red.

I piss blood
  drip blood
  miss blood
when food isn't
enough to survive.

Inevitable Lust

Inevitable lust
invades lost consciousness,
I wish the world would end today.

Dark shadow clouds gather above my damaged skull.
Clustering scattered moths infest the vanishing stratosphere;
idiots leading idiots telling sarcastic horny jokes
about white women's artificial breasts.

The city is growing uncontrollably,
nobody knows where they are going.

Selfishness is virtue of the invisible artist;
to paint with words no one hears
makes bashful pride hunger for premature
death.

Buddhist Monks suck impotent dicks of
Baptist Reverends during Easter's indoctrinated séance.

Bodies cripple what menial potential
the human being might've thought it possessed
at one instance of escaped thought.
Existence is the mold you see on the planet
when viewing outer space photographs.

Caged Animal Love

I will be alone forever.

I weep every time I examine your torpid body with derelict flesh.

You have me in a whirlwind mess,
vainglorious mythological palimpsest;
I carve my torment in your detrimental nourishment.

In darkness we conspire genocide, cardiac incineration creates occult
practices waltzing nostalgic poltergeist, brutalize blindfolded eyes
wicked corrupted seamstress mending intense closeness to nothingness.
Blessed lover over tourniquet quenchless deprivation scandalous
blossoming malevolent flowers shimmering crystal meth injected
into newborn babies neutralizing agonizing pain worse than molten
crowbars jammed into bleeding rectum.

The only way I can live without you is when I exercise insubordination.
Sanity is a pillow for the masses. I decapitate calico kittens to
substitute lack of wasting time with your archetype. Twenty-first century
millennium nightmares safeguarded with capitalist interests enslaving
static selves wistful fantasies astonishing exultation for crucified saints,
martyred Jesuits draped in fluorescent cassocks...

you reveal yourself to me in your evil.

I hate you like I hate God.

You have condemned us to suffer without reason, without
    comprehension.

All I ever desired was to love you and your creation. You mock me with indifference and hypocrisy looking into my soul finding everything you ever needed and ignoring it with idiosyncratic stupidity admonishing an absurd world where mechanical technology dehumanizes us where lust is the only preoccupation where the dullness of my words remain on computer screens inoperative co-opted by empty wallets and unfulfilled existence; calm fury distorted blurred vision cruelty virtuous like hierarchy natural selection.

I worship in ritual solitary.

You are becoming habitual to an ex drug addict and premature alcoholic. I dread the moment we depart each other's presence. I wanted to be left alone to die in isolation painting portraits with meaningless words where no one could venture.
You are as sullen as deformed sculptures.

I am dying.

I hate the world and hate the life and hate the tumultuous premonitions of a future wife never married. If I ever had children I'd murder them after the abortion was performed. Our connection is deformed.

I am dying.

Lying to you every second
exults your undeserving being
to echelons of heaven's bashful retreat.
If I handed you a dozen roses on Villaintine's Day I'd piss on them
    beforehand.
I'd rather tongue you with veins bulging, massaging your immature
    whereabouts under your dirty anus used like inebriated sentiments
    in cigar-infested lounges,
the stench of your confused aura

I have no faith.

...the world is ending
We keep pretending...
...condescending one another
Put the gun to your twitching lips...
...let me chew your flatulent tits
Belong to an organization of misfits...
...lampshade philosophy
Rope choking neck...
...own my utter disrespect
The god I killed...
...the bill I never paid
The idea of getting laid...
...is much better than
an unexpected police raid.

I'm preoccupied with ego like everyone else.
I want to see you as often as the raven screams.
I want to fuck you and touch you and suck you
and love you and give you everything you never really dreamed.
I don't want to see you every day.
The pain is bearable, the distance unfathomable,
the dance un-learnable.

I was going to purchase a diamond ring for you today but noticed a
homeless bum on the streets begging for change and bought him a
drink instead.
I am friends only with the dead.
They are the only ones that know how to forgive.
When I stare at you I hate the fact that life is unfair.
I am quite familiar with the skeletons you attempt to share.

I laugh.

I know everything there isn't to know.
I know nothing of the late December snow evaporating
over mercurial lakes caused by man-made earthquakes.
Our pseudo relationship is celibate,
infrequently practicing sodomy on bunny rabbits.

I saunter into the confessional, pronounce to the shrouded priest on the
other side that I used to be homosexual, violently masturbating, focusing
on the father and the son and the holy spirit while he sermonizes us
into submission from the pulpit coming all over the dirty Eucharist.

The Epitome of Stupidity

You're all a bunch of brainwashed motherfuckers!
Partying like you can afford it, dancing without rhythm,
Smoking cigarettes like they was prohibited,
Doing what you are told.

                    I'm way too fuckin old for your
                         petty power play.

I ain't nobody's fucking slave!
I'm more intelligent than your stupid ways.

Love Your Oppressor

I love my oppressor
so much that I will kill him.

My primary oppressor is the
white devil cave dwelling barbarian cracker gringo
that possesses no soul.

You do not frighten me any more.

I can fight back like 10 million South Africans
violently demonstrating in Johannesburg.
You cannot change my history with
scientific ethnocentric propaganda
like the Kennewick Man.

Just because your cranium radius extends
longer does not mean you are physically,
mentally nor spiritually stronger;
it means you're inferior.

Hate Those That Hate You

The world needs to end.
nothing more to defend.
you act like my friend then try to bring me to an end.
you condescend, go start a new trend for all the sheep to follow,
bowing to a temple all the lies you swallow.
from wigwams to napalm,
Nintendo to church psalms,
everything is wrong,
the strong no longer have room to think;
intelligence is on the brink of extinction.
felicity is a contaminated city of correctional facilities.
I pursue the impossibility of possibly establishing
an organization of colored conspiracies.
Fuck Whitey!
they don't know how to fight,
every single one of you is an unsightly adversarial foe.
I'm a vanquished Zapatista,
you're just another Baptist preacher advocating the virtues of capitalism;
don't tell me what I already know!
life for brown people everywhere in Amerika is prison!
racism is a fringe benefit for university students learning and leading
the unstoppable movement of Anglo Saxon supremacy disguised as
    apology!
your media monopoly distorts the truth.
educational hypocrisy incarcerates our youth.
white kids comprise 75% of the student body on all college campuses
    while the reverse is true for black and hispanic people doing bids.
now take a long look under my sleepless eyelids.
do you really think a bunch of white environmentalists are gonna save
    the planet they continue to destroy with arrogant, selfish lifestyles of
    materialistic obsession?
The lesson to learn is not scientific;
The solution is very specific;
return all lands to indigenous native descendants.

Troublemaker

The young child grows into a man,
it's impossible to understand what's
going on in this universe it's like we're
cursed, can death be any worse? Me
first and you still end up last; people
living for the future only traveling towards
the past. I'm a cast away like Tom Hanks
but ain't no Hollywood skank like him
and Hilary Swank. It's reality driving me
towards insanity. What an iniquitous
calamity those telling me not to use
profanity. Who the fuck died and
made you omnipotent? Your impotent
self-righteousness doesn't make you
enlightened superfluous with so-called
consciousness. Pontius Pilate! Scrubbing
your filthy imperialist hands of somebody
else's responsibility. Diligence, determination,
and discipline shall carry me beyond
your ignorant worldly impossibilities
and subordinate biological capabilities.
Casualties of ignominious war will
continue to accumulate while we wish
to debate the military industrial hate
keeping us sedate. How late can we
wait to dominate our ungrateful fate
before other members of humanity's
untroubled depravity holler
check mate?

Killer of Religion

I'm the killer of religion
Speak with distorted precision
Design nuclear weapon laboratory centers
While worshipping the whore of the Christian
Condemned to a bonfire of planetary delusion
It's all chaos and confusion
Perception, ideas, belief, faith, and decision
Watch me fuck your God
Occupy your land like Amerikan soldiers
Committing premeditated sadistic acts of torture
Abandoned in Babylon
Blonde hair, blue-eyed demon
Choking on my own semen
Watching the temple of Jerusalem
Topple only to be resurrected in the form
Of a Fourth Reich Nazi Jewish reincarnation
Listen to the black magic incantation
Scientologists, psychologists practicing
Occult type destructive physics—retaliate to reclaim my fate
Sacrifice my children strapped with a vest of explosives
To show the international world that no one cares
Spare me your self-righteous proclamations of an eye for an eye
Visions of Gandhi left me blind before birth
My mission is to desecrate this forbidden Earth
Hidden cryptography, biblical encryption decoded through
Computer globalization purchased through capitalistic manipulation
The teachings of Jesus taught us to submit
The only thing we learned in school was how to quit
Shit—I don't need the approval of mankind
My fellow kind of man unkind, to justify my existence as a ghostwriter
searching

For complicated language like Russian, Chinese, Arabic, and Spanglish
I'm trapped forever in a chamber imbued with white supremacy
If you ain't Anglo-Saxon you just a smut villain slave wasting away
waiting for the day to discover a better way to expedite your predestined
fatalistic decay
But you can think you're important as 7 billion people compete for
space
Simultaneously creating 300,000 replications 24/7
The human species is a disgrace, creating perpetual wars to see who can
make it to Heaven. We thirst for wisdom, power, sex, and wealth
Ignoring imagination as she speaks to us about spiritual health
Stealth bombs, Apache helicopters, M-16 advanced weaponry is as
Deadly as biological warfare: the virus of AIDS, SARS, and a brand new
lethal flu
Fuck you!—the only expression of the final generation.
Life is intoxicated apparition.

The System

I sense all the jealous snakes acting fake,
condense the life sentence given to me since incomprehensible birth.
There is no mirth on Earth, for what it isn't worth
I still plan to burn down every church.
My Christian hypocrisy is synonymous with
Western European devil worshipping philosophy.
Like Soren, Bertrand, Jean-Paul Sartre,
life is worthless from the start;
heart is what's needed to supercede the omnipresent darkness;
Determination will annihilate the Apartheid States
stating they're united, divided we fall when one hears
the call of personal advancement in an
asylum of materialistic enchantment.
Pray introversive for children of this forsaken
planet dying of AIDS & Cancer;
no matter how bad it gets I won't submit
to the self-aggrandized Germanic race Chancellor.

Point your guns down toward the ephemeral snow.
Imperialism is someone praising what you know.

For my fugitive companeros
lay low,
      walk brisk,
           talk to no one about nothing.
Keep moving
      as long
          as
               sunshine
          stands
      still.

Abolish the prison system with a melted tear.
My incentive to heal has wandered.
The criminal suspect is the one sporting a
uniform with a shiny badge depicting suicidal pride.

Relinquish the iniquity of prejudice and injustice.
Plain and sorrowful.
        Pain tomorrow,
brother can I borrow a nickel
for a red star and yellow sickle?

No More Birthdays

I don't blame the God that doesn't exist for my mistaken creation.
Crucified in the delivery room during midnight made a forsaken
abortion see the dark light as it blinded my eternally sick soul.
So what if the world continues to bleed.
Does this mean we shall overcome the coveted blessings
of Earthly greed? At god's speed shall insightful demons
steal our hopes of misleading dreams.

Pain and comfort, tingling and feelings no longer there;
I really don't care...
I truly can't care anymore for the herpetic sores
that are 7 billion humans wasting in an uncouth spherical toilet.
I scratch my ailing testicles, sniff my index finger, relish
the fetish discharge of opium, organic green tea, fried feces,
and salty vagina mixed up underneath the hemorrhoidal rectum.

Time moves fast not fast enough though faster than the fastest could
ever fathom.

I don't need twenty-five more years of confusion;
Twenty-five years until the end in the beginning;
Twenty-five moments of crying out to a subliminally
egoistic parasitic populace that remains conspiratorially deaf;
Twenty-five intentional years moving backwards
to my ultimate goal of suicide.
Twenty-five years without enough time.

I think of suicide everyday...
a one-way ticket to a few eternities of isolation...
the end of re-discovered innocence...

Depression looms inside a house
of twisted spider webs holding broken wine bottles
after the revolution failed again and again and again…
Begin to bargain with the devil;
Jesus searches for my disappearing soul
under an aluminum mask with missing eyes.
Fornicating curtains cover stem-cell embryos,
another used tampon for the executive decisions
ruining people's evil lives:

there is NO DEMOCRACY
there is NO JUSTICE
there is NO EGALITARIANISM
there is NO GOLDEN RULE—ONLY RULES
there is NO ADEQUATE HEALTH CARE
there is NO FREE ENTERPRISE, FREE SPEECH, FREE ASSEMBLY
there is NO FREEDOM
there is NO KNOWLEDGE
there is NO EDUCATION BUT MANIPULATION THROUGH DOMINAITON
there is NO MONEY, ONLY CAPITAL CURRENCY KNOWN AS CAPITAL
PUNISHMENT FOR NO MONEY HAVING HUNGRY MINORITY WHORES
there is NO GOD, NO PROPHETS, NO SAINTS, NO ANGELS, NO HEAVEN
        ONLY HELL
there is NO UNDERSTANDING
there is NO LAW
there is NO WEALTH
there is NO FRATERNITY
there is NO SORORITY, BUT YES, MANY A SORARATE
there is NO SPIRITUALITY—DEAD SOULS THOUGH, ASK GOGOL
there is NO RELIGION YOU IDIOTIC INFIDELIC TURBANS AND
CHRISTIANS
there is NO PEACE
there is NO FAITH
there is NO RESPONSIBILITY UNLESS TAKEN BY IRRESPONSIBLE
RESPONSES
        ON RELATIONSHIPS IN REPOSE
there is NO MONOGAMY NOR MARRIAGE

there is NO REMEDY
there is NO MEDICINE
there is NO LOYALTY
there is NO ORDER
there is NO ORGANIZATION
there is NO COOPERATION, JUST CORPORATIONS
there is NO HELP
there is NO DIALECTICS
there is NO PRIVACY
there is NO MOBILITY
there is NO ONE LEFT
there is NO DESTINY
there is NO SALVATION
there is NO HOPE
there is NO LOVE, NO LOVE, NO LOVE
        because LOVE is considered to be a lonely emotion…

there is no love.

I'm not as cynical as a metaphysical
thirteen year-old virgin that has AIDS.

The truth is used.
Ridges of lice,
catacombs filed inside-out,
half dogs, half wolves dripping
discarded plasma,
the sun changes light severity without asking.

Nothing is mine and no one is owned.
The mockingbird dies,
The blackbird craves and crows,
butterflies sting the skin
like a swarm of cannibalistic African killer bees.
Sing to me restless guitar,
Slap my face father,
Shun my shame mother,

Shine my shoe nigger,
Suck my dick world,
Sin my sun daughter,
Sodomize me Sade,
Sing my song Sade,
the day carries on in a bad way.

Your scientific madness encapsulates dormant minds—
powers of delusion capture corrugated flesh—
Your suggestion is meaningless.
Your sex appeal dies with every day's dawn—
Your pagan rituals have my blessings—
Your attitude is brand new—
I too desire to smell the hue
of a decomposing wilderness
made only for a few.

Flow like saliva
from the white glossy corners
of your thirsty mouth.

Demons keep wanting to molest me.

I'm frightened,
terrified about tonight's
fascinating dreamscape.

My heroes are the murderous images
flashing before my mind,
the kind strangers.

Distortion,
futuristic oracles bring forth
a portion of miracles lost in a world…

A world full of corruption,
A world without perfection,

A world where infectious flies
eat shit of the first serving of the sky.

The ways of Satan catapult this maze of twisted lust
that bursts wide open the hope haunting my inner disgust.

People should stop believing in their self-justified lies...
Everybody needs to commit suicide.

On A Trip

sniff-sniff...Holy shit! I feel like I'll never quit. Just one more hit PLEASE! just one fuckin hit. Dat's it. Nothing like an upper before an elitist supper. Makes me feel like one cool white motherfucker. No eats, just wanna sit, stay seated, drink vino and neurotically assimilate amongst these gringos. Friends. Roman Descendants. Fellow Santa Feans. Fellow Decadents! Don't mind me, I'm just enjoying you not enjoying me enjoying the fact I'm not enjoying my life. So—SILENCE—the members of our dinner party fall prey to the cast of shadowing. Keep looking over your shoulders cocklickers—HyPoCrItEs! Eclectic Spics such as we don't need to see beyond our own hypocrisy. See? Leaving so soon are you? Perhaps chap, if your ass wasn't so tight it would clap. Maybe if your ninety year-old wanna-be nineteen wife didn't look like she wanted to FUCK ME! Well...yeah. The room has cleared in less than half an hour. What power! What audacity that our capacity is more tenacious than tenacity given to minority mediocrity. This is a DEMOn MockRACey after all, que no, or no, no? Suppose shall say some see us succumb so suddenly like Susan soothin a blow job harder than the hardest hard as hard can get yet set some stupid sonofabitch so soon scowling surreptitiously seething snake-like secretions slipping smoothly down my thigh. Yes. No. So? Luckily I showed up late. Dinner almost over yet? I'll drink another glass. Dinner over. YES! But who will pay the bill? But who will pay the bill? Again—but Who will Pay The bill? Not I said blind crack head with a glass pipe in the eye. The best thing about living in an ultra capitalistic capitalist capitalism universe is that no one has to pay for anything in order to frolic frantically down to the jamboreeeeeeeeeeeeeeeeeeeeeeeeeeeeeeeeeeee! Eee No. Did you see the way I just Peed. Meee-o-my I feel like getting extremely, customarily, traditionally, exceptionally, expediently, HIGH HIGH HIGH HIGH, my, my, my. More drink, More drug, More pussy, pussy, pussy here pussypussypussypussy. Pass dat leno before da lina like I love this. WHOooooeeeeeee! Enter Bar. Accept ecstasy. Another beer. Another shot. One more toke. Cigarette Time. Oh Shit! Here it is. Yup. I knew this would come again. Hit the toilet Kid. Sit down on it Kid. No more eats at that stupid fuckin fucked-up foul servin shit on no wheels SUB. Fuck UNM—Uniformity for Niggers and Mexicans—or—Under education for Nitwits and Meshuggeners. Aagghh! Yeaaahhh, Fuck Yeah! Now I'm feeling it. Tingly inside, my noierves, my noierves—I can feel every one of my last single little brittle noierves. Time is no time not like the time I felt time but the time of no time. Time is essence in time of essence with no essence cuz essence can suck my dick—HA! Time. Time to find a chick to try and stick my dick in. Only dick has really, really—No—REALLY shriveled up like if I just ascended from a swimming pool filled with two tons of ice. No sex tonight. Thank God. Fuck up my trip anyhows. I'm moving. I'm shakkkking. I'm fidgeting like Julia Roberts getting hotly bothered by motley Richard Queer in that Pretty Woman-like romantic fantasy fuck. Heart's pounding—Bah boom, bah boom bah boom bah boom, Bah boom bah boom bah boom Bah boom. Settle down, it's only a trip, a moment. Think, Think, Think! NO, don't think. Take a breath— INHAAAAAALE—exHAAAAAAAAAAALE. Good. Bah boom badda boom badda boom baddabadda baddabada boom baddaboom badda—Fuck I'm dying. Oh fuck—FUCK FUCK FUCK, I DON'T WANNA DIE (yeah you do) so why not prepare. Whoa. Okay. You can get off the toilet now. I don't think I'll get used to that. Still quivering like a dildo. Walking on air, on cloudy air in dingy piss aroma 6 X 8 shithole in nothing near a classy tavern. Mirror. SPLASH of cold water on spongy face. Pupils as big as Plain M & M hard-shell candy. Sit down (what I just happened to want to do all happy night). Sit down. Smoke. There she is. The girl I've been sorta dating sorta not dating cuz I wanted to fuck her, but have yet to fuck her, but don't want to fuck her anymore. This latter part cuz I've grown to respect her. Like her. One of the few girls I've actually shared an interesting time and mutual conversation with. NOTE: Never fuck a girl you like; not to mention she's white. I gotta get away from her. She won't leave me alone. Thank that non-existent god I don't know her well enough to want to spend any more moments with her than I already have. Be nice. Yes I'll walk you to your car—Thank that no god—Bye, bye—yes, you too. Back to the clubhouse, feeling like an angel who can't fly. Unaware of my humanity is freedom. Goddamn it! The Fuzz. Shit.

Let me see. Here's the equation: White establishment with more than mostly white patrons where everybody's getting fucked-up on mostly other than liquor white stuff plus fat-ass white sergeant commanding mostly short shit skin colored systematized soldiers—problem: who will they bust?—better to stay away for a moment—do—return—eventually. Low and behold; two dumbass spics sitting handcuffed in the back of a roller for underage drinking. It's a good thing they don't bust all them upper-class creamy community civilians snorting mountains and mountains of capped snow. Good thing my skin is more Caucasoid than indigenous. Good thing I speaka da Englixh vwery vwery articulatorynessly. Oh well. WOW! Who's she? Looks like the poifect type: brown, thirty something, horny, and I'm sure a mother of more than one kid. Hi. What's your name? (Not that I'd remember). I'm Gregory. No, from San Antonio. I've lived in Denver for the past twelve years. The best thing about talking to strange women is the cool lies you get to tell them. Well, they're not really lies, more like not-so-truthful facts and events. So, you look pretty well pie-eyed, been here long? Let's dance. She takes my hand and allows me to rub up on her like if sexual harassment was still legal. We kiss, fondle, talk more bullshit. I ask for her number, she gives me a cell one—probably false. She asks for mine, I give her it reluctantly. She's about to pass out. I could probably fuck her but luckily for us I'm not quite into copulating with drunkards when they're flamboyantly inebriated. Not to mention my prick is hiding somewhere. Just two children! Now that's ecstasy.

Pussy In Your Mouth

Marcel! Marcel!

The dog catcher
shoulda found the tramp
when his master left the gate
secured enough for thieves.

Slyness
and
finesse
is no less
the feat
of four feet
into
dead meat.

Meet Mongo Monster Mongrel Meticulously Masturbating Moving
Miraculous Mountains Momentously Mendaciously Manipulating...

MEEEOOOWWWWW!

Aw fuck.
The cat in the hat got stuck.

August 30, 2000   3:27pm:

The trials of human survival are ultimately dehumanizing. This afternoon as I was dismounting the bus at my regular stop before walking home, I encountered a peculiar individual who seemed to be following me. At least that's what my instinctive paranoia was telling me.

It began on the trip home to my final stop. I was seated towards the front of the bus because I'm a virgin bus passenger who still hasn't developed a trust for the rear of the vehicle, considering I'm still quite new to the urban center of 'Burque. Nevertheless, about two to three miles away from my destination, this short, skinny, bald-headed cross-eyed dirty bastard sits in front of me and begins to stare. At first, I avoided all eye contact with the scamp in the hopes of not generating any kind of conversation. Luckily for me, my hopes never fall through. About five minutes into his obsession with me, he commences to attempt to talk to me:

SCAMP: What school do you go to?

Obviously my backpack and juvenile demeanor must've given my secret away. I didn't respond.

SCAMP: Where do you go to school?
ME: *(barely audible)* Over there that way.
SCAMP: Oh.

I was beginning to feel nauseated. Don't you just despise it when someone tries talking to you on one of those days when your tongue is in hibernation? I deliberately answered in a mumbled tone to shut him up. Fortunately for him, he acted as if he understood me.

SCAMP: Do you like it there?

"Shut the fuck up and don't look at me as if I'm some sixteen year-old hooker with a wet white T-shirt on" is what I felt like telling him. I didn't have the balls to do so. I still don't. I'm unsure why, but I can never really be unkind to people unless they do something severely drastic to me. I just don't possess a knack for being unpleasant, even to the uttermost unpleasantries. After some minutes of uncomfortable silence and my pathetic attempts at avoiding eye contact with him, I think he got the hint. Although, I could tell through my peripheral vision that he was still glancing at me from time to time. I wanted to bitch slap him.

The bus was finally nearing my stop. As I grabbed my backpack by the straps, I noticed the little fuck was eyeballing me again. He got up from his seat, knowing I was about to get off the bus. I knew right then that he must be following me. The bus stopped and he was in front of me when we dismounted. I was about to stay on until the next stop but I felt too lazy to walk an extra five hundred or so feet to my house. Leave it up to laziness to fuck up your world. Immediately after the bus departed he began again:

SCAMP: What kind of hobbies do you like?
ME: Huh?
SCAMP: *(walking alongside me in my direction)* What kind of hobbies are you interested in?
ME: I'm not.

I was starting to be unpleasant.

SCAMP: What's your name?

That was it! This shit had gone on too long. I clenched my left fist, the weaker of the two, in preparation of disfiguring his face. It's not that he was crude, rude, or mean, or even that he was life threatening (so it seemed), but this line of questioning was too shady coming from a complete stranger that I had no desire of knowing in the first place. To tell you the truth, he didn't appeal to me as the type of person I would befriend or want to take a *first* look at.

ME: James.

It took me about a lifetime of two seconds to come up with that ingenious false identity. He told me his name was Hank, or John, or Bill, or some fuckin uninteresting title. I wasn't paying attention. All I wanted to do was leave his presence. I started walking faster.

SCAMP: Nice to meet you.

He held out his left palm. Time froze. I wasn't sure what I should do. I figured if I didn't shake his hand, he might get offended and pull out a knife or gun and try to kill me right there. If I did shake his hand, he might pass-on lice or some skin disease or something or other that would physically harm me.

ME: Likewise.

As usual I reacted instead of acted. His palm felt dry, crusty, and cold.

ME: Later.

I crossed the street, knowing he couldn't keep up with me. I went out of my customary path in order to lose him. Finally, he disappeared.

Upon my return home, my thoughts went a little something like this:

> Damn Angelo, you're one cruel fuck! What the hell is wrong with you? Why do you constantly tell yourself not to judge people, but then you invariably do all the time. Poor guy. I bet he was just trying to make a friend. I suppose it's no coincidence that the poor are always the loneliest. I hate this city! *(looking over both shoulders)* Fucker better not be following me. Aw shit. I feel bad. Fuck dat! You know better. You can't trust no one, NO ONE! Still, I don't think he meant me any harm. Never can tell though. He was probably some fag who thought I was cute and wanted to take me home, if he has a home that is. Then again, he was probably just looking for someone to talk to. I bet nobody's paid him any mind in years. Why are people like that? Why am I like that? It's no different when you're on the streets

and some dude comes up and asks if you got a few bucks or change to spare, he hasn't eaten in days. And you tell him nothing, continue walking as an apparition he were...walking along with at least five to ten bucks in your grip. Every passing second we are separating ourselves from each other, especially yourself. Nobody gives a shit about anyone. I'll never understand why some people suffer more than others. And why someone can have all the greatest and kindest intentions in the world, but never give an ounce of consideration back to the world. Give nothing back. Humans are the lowest form of life roaming the universe. All the power of greatness in the world and most of us don't have a clue what to do with it. I feel bad. Fuck guilt. Guilt never got anyone anywhere. Only you can change the world kid, only you. Your kindness does no good incarcerated in your soul. Matter of fact that's what I call evil. Aw...fuck this. Who gives a shit? The world will move, he'll keep going and so will you. There's no justification in what you just did, nor is there any redemption. Life is what it is...

I'm aware that what I did was wrong, but I've never been one to do anything correctly. There are just too many damn people on this Earth to try and know all of them, even some of them. I don't have time for anyone, much less myself. But, how you treat others is how you treat yourself. As I picture him thereafter, I can definitely see my reflection. The reflection of a child-like being who has yet to grow-up, and who has yet to understand anything. There's no hope in an individual world that will not share. The more I think about this incident, the more I admire people like him, and despise those like me.

Desperation IV

I hurt,
but
I can't
flirt
with
death.

Book II
Lamentation

Soulless Woman

I made love to the devil...
      and it was beautiful.

Some Corny Ass Shit to Say to a Lonely Older Woman as She's Crying Over Her Failing Second Marriage

The world is suffering, *serenity*
but so do we.

All that is great
you cannot see.

Your beautiful feelings
of fear belong
to a forgetful moment's hour;

 Regret nothing…

Love is the only power.

Portrait of a Woman

Undressing you is an excursion...

      urging to ejaculate an immaculate burgeon of persuasions
cavalcading consistent diversions persisting from vouchsafed persons
cursing the caution often associated with a plethora of pneumatic
addicts on sacrilegious sabbaticals thinking what they should feel feeling
what thoughts got caught in a tight situation like a knot but ought the
elation determine surreal occasions blazon' amazon' phases of dazes
tainted by vermin germinating inner warfare similar to dinner dates
eating plates and crates as hate overthrows a side of suicide realized
through subliminalized fates while mates activate tears of dread tears of
loath tears of pride tears of mine tears benign to the mind activity of
creativity as gravity actively elevates our state of being to seeing mortal
fatality a reality driven from priority cause given minorities digress for
stress immersed in perverse motives of diverse vehicles common to
all who call late nights early mornings adoring forlorn material objects
of desire higher than fowl who scowl at the howl of an insomniac
owl's growl like the hunger of the younger individual more intellectual
residual perpetual effectual confessional than a pulpit of professional
impetuosity worse than Dostoevsky's ground under thunder always
leaves a blunder whimsical like wonder funner than sex.

Whispers caress our essence, a slipped breath left to lather you lavishly
with lotion like relishment, an embellishment cherished for the
passionate instance of patience, Alas! acquiescence blesses this desolate
with soothing solace of presence.

I Know A Womyn

I know a womyn...
  dying in an inferno of lighthearted sorrow,
   ensconced in the past, avoiding tomorrow.

She picks dried flowers from swollen sullen eye sockets
  of dead politicians,
  kisses the self-inflicted wounds of black magicians.
Caresses the paralysis
  of my lacerated heart,
  shows me where it ends, where it starts;
   the perpetual bleeding,
   the pleading for mercy,
  she sticks contaminated needles into my breastplate,
  spits saliva in my mouth when I am thirsty.
She plays hopscotch, jump rope, and holds hands
  with children that never existed,
  regrets the fact that she never resisted;
   the temptations of the flesh,
   the spiritual mess of this forgotten world—
   rotten womynhood robbed her of the little innocent girl.
This womyn is a teardrop...
  dropping from a ripped eyelash,
  soaking skin with sour impulses,
leaving a trail of Basquiat's frustrated brush stroke;
   punished throughout life with poverty,
   content intentionally remaining broke.
Such a cruel joke,
  the loneliness of such a saint;
  I watch her desperately attempt to
  color the dawn's neoplastic hallucination
  with truth, peace, justice—invisible paint.
I know her,
  I see her,
   I feel her
    dancing with my skeleton

on top of hollow graveyards.
I sniff her,
      touch her,
           listen to her
                tickle a hypocritical gentleman
                    making love to a shallow depraved
bard.
I know a womyn...
      laughing internally at the stupidity of mankind
           searching for that feeling of your first high,
              only to reveal there's really nothing there to
find.

She drives me insane
      with her original smile,
      with her psychotic wayward ways of partying all night;
Yet, just to be with her again,
      all the apocalyptic tyrants in the world, alone, I would fight.
I'd face racist discrimination,
confront hostile demonization,
embrace biological deterioration,
if it meant that ultimate realization.

Her skin is as soft as a kind of blue Miles Davis seducing his subtle
horn...
I know this womyn—a womyn forlorn,
                a womyn scorned,
                    a womyn torn,
                        a womyn born.

      She infects me with anxiety,
      stresses me with insomnia I can never cure;
I've never met a womyn like this,
      a womyn with surrendered eyes and a soul impure.
I'm not sure who she is,
I really don't know her very well,
the slightest thought of her punishes me severely here in my

comfortable hell.
I can tell I'll never bathe with her in the imaginary springs
    of untrammeled mountain air,
        I don't care,
at least once I was fortunate enough to lose myself
    in the fortunes of her surreal, ethereal hair.
This womyn tames bonfires in the hopes of insurrection,
losing the memory of her name in dope, perfect in her imperfections.
Her voice races the unforgiving wind around the never-ending ends of
the planet,
when she speaks she's more melodic than Benny's clarinet or Mozart's
final nonet,
her hazardous apparition I just can't forget.
I know a womyn...
cohort of naked jackals, stripping a snake from its scales.
I know a womyn...
collector of demolished dreams, practitioner of betrayal.
Eternal meditating Santeria minister, sister to sinister behavior,
perhaps this misplaced womyn is my talismanic absent savior.
There is no remedy for a yearning so pervasive,
I'm just now learning the meaning of togetherness evasive.
There's not a persuasive word to use to heal her abused trust,
I must persist and resist the calamity to easily give-up.
I sense her,
        move her,
                lose her
                        to nocturnal emissions;
I fear her,
        care for her
                and dare her
                        to proceed without permission.
I know her...
        she sleeps with terrorists underground;
        carved caved getaways, paradise slumber
        we are all just a number anyways.
I enslave her...
        whipping her neck with dirty jagged fingernails

scratching the ocean of her lamenting body,
phenomenal lust inferior to her enchanting personality.
I know a womyn...
she doesn't live in reality,
she's lost like a Mexican child in Juarez begging tourists for
impossibility,
she's the ostracized, the outcast, the renegade wandering
purposeless,
surviving outside plainclothes society.
I watch her
pierce her wrists with an eagle's endangered feather,
she speaks of drugs, wine and sleeping forever.
I know a womyn...
hanging out with untouchable shadows,
smoking stale cigarettes
and not giving a fuck...
I know a womyn...
unenthusiastically meandering through life
on two broken feet, running from damnation,
running out of luck.
I know a womyn...
she gathers pennies on polluted streets and
gives them to hungry people; she's oppressed by forces good
and evil.
I know a womyn...
her tears are blood, her poetry is requiem, her hands were
made to heal;
I know a womyn...
her fears are done, her sophistry is opium, she plans to stay
silent and kneel.

Her violent massage gave me an idea to construct a collage of her
baby pictures with photos of her future and put them in a place where
nobody can see,

I know a womyn...
she's the type of womyn that makes me want to believe.

I want someone to believe in me

Accidental Moments

While the crimson shaded fluid flowed and squirted every beat,
heat usurped my consciousness like overdosing LSD,
entering permanent oasis without a pass.
Faces became distant places more remote
than fantasies of adolescent innocence.
Reflecting, shining fragments of Plexiglas pierced within my wrist,
a twist of destiny got the best of me; remain still
for the sake of breathing breathlessly seeing seething
liquid soak my dreams. Frailty impales me...
sets me adrift swift ecstasies of agony known as
b-l-i-s-s extending a k-i-s-s.
Chattering, indiscernible, no lamentations or exclamations
of concern for one who doesn't learn. The intern medic
sticks his finger inside my lacerated cavity
and flicks the wilted tendons;
a solid rise of scar tissue
tells me all the time
to crack the
stiffness of
forsaken
touch.

Instruments of
riveting vibes
racing up and down
around my frame
with no recognizable name
committing transgressions of
electricity beyond complacent felicity,
such as the first time it happened.
The drowsy effect produced
strokes the air flying towards
the center of Earth,

an addition to bleeding
yourself. The shadowed plasma emits
an odor that turns stomachs,
gliding fingers through my hair
glancing oculars of forgiveness
grimacing expressions of hopelessness
allowed me to feel like I wasn't alone.
A palm was there to grip tightly—
A thoughtless utterance to calm the outcries—
A choice to rejoice in the pleasure of evading fear;
Years later I would come to regret it.

Listening to Tom Waits In Psychiatric Ward Gloom

when the world ends...
I wanna be cradled by the scintillating aroma
        of your bloodshot restlessness,
suffer the vulgar fascination of our mutual ruin...

Condemned to this abandoned schoolyard institutional playground
of dying trees, crying seas, and lying bourgeoisie,
we the forever deceived perceive to ruthlessly feed off
Kierkegaardian dread—
        wakened vagabonds
        breathlessly treading scatological destruction,
        heretically searching for phantasmagoric resurrection,
as the terrorized dead battle to taste
the last wasted physiological construction murdered
from unseasoned butchered decapitated cattle,
impetuously decomposing inside derogatory intestines,
chanting soft Satanic hymns.

Little jovial bashful hand twisted mechanical puppets—
        prostrate your tattered limbs beneath my burden;
            Listen to the wonderful glistening of
                evaporating snowflakes melting with the
                    unassailable sun—

I shall not have fun in this morose existence
if I'm not to detain your secret vulnerability,
your sacrificial pain my evil beloved fugitive wind.

Nervous glitter shadow movement,
lighthearted candle flicker,
obsession possess this hedonistic vision—
fall victim to the plastic condition.

Induced schizophrenia to mask fragmented sorrows,
vibrating nuclear bulldozer demolishes future,
haunt my lineal reality after tomorrow pretends,
mercilessly drenched in cocaine showers,
molested through time borrowed,
the shape-shifting power structured Leviathan.

I am the hidden angel forbidden to taste your electromagnetic touch,
      the devoured lame duck running out of insurrectionary
filibusters;
my decrepit heart stops upon delicate thoughts of you,
  my rotting toothpick legs furiously shiver to savor your convalescent
    aura.
November's chilled evening susurrations establish intimate converse
    between
      mother Africa's sleeping immune deficient percussions and
          one of Puccini's drifting voices belonging to a
          turnstone mistress seeking pleasant distress.

Pompous as a lead violinist,
I shall overwhelm you with reverence,
    not with lustful affection.

Provocative, bewitching as you appear,
    the fear of losing your unreal beauty
      scorns me to relinquish distrustful erections.

      Unconventional like Duchamp aesthetics
      immersed in mordacious Brechtian perversity.

Where is my Emma?
  My lonely desolate desperate Bovary
    waltzing in an immortal arsenic swamp,
      daydreaming about that life not endured by poverty-vowed
      saints.
      My defiant, insubordinate Goldman building bombs
          to appropriate from the rich what they greedily fleece
              from us;

[handwritten annotation: to be reworded as a whole / of / lusted as a lady / is to love more completely]

shedding wizdom passing pamphlets confounding corrupt cops
    shooting totalitarian fascist capitalists swift as a
        toy Manchester terrier; steal barricades and iron barriers
        shall never incarcerate the misinterpreted truth.

Where is my Virginia?
    The lamenting wolf scavenging the intimidating past,
      enduring step-brothers putting it up your ass without
          permission,
        raping you into submission like right-wing ideology
          transformed
      into public policy, permanently damaging your fragile
          psychology;
      no redemption nor recourse but the merciless river to
          drown
    unapologetic tears.

      Too many fears, not enough strength.

Where is my Sylvia?
    Prepensely shoving her emasculating lunatic crown
      into a pre-heated oven, duct taping breathing space
        between the door
      and kitchen floor to protect your sleeping
        children upstairs
    without making a sound…
    all grown-up and nowhere to go except down.

Poetry is a cheap hooker bitch that'll suck your prickly puss espousing
dick for government handout cheese but still lack the decency to retract
her needle pinching teeth and cap her undervalued dignified cavities...

Where is my Judy?
    My garland of pill popping extravagance,
      abusing Thoreauvian and Emersonian anarchist transcendence;

    I sabotage your evanescent soul with tenuous kisses.

Where is my Liza?
My Minnelli exploding potent operatic vocals
from the mouth of a stampeded mouse playing possum;
kinetic thespian ham attempting to seduce my offensive
imagination.
My Liza, my ontological muse that doesn't have to be naked
to arouse my diffident suspicions.

You are one to adore.

You will only have me when you want me:
You will only want me when you know me:
You will only know me when you need me:
You will only need me when I am no more.

Tribute

God always tries to act out Robert De Niro, but
only heroes rival political y religious fame,
a bull that rages suffocates the atmosphere tame
Sorry! Apologies are awards for apologetic claims,
      Taxi driver turn pimp, midnight runs throughout an abysmal hole.

Deer becomes hunter decorated in military attire, yet
poor St. Christopher was seen walking down a narrow steep,
Kings of comedy greet a barrel at age thirty-eight just to meet
Awakenings; a Cuban wetback plus the callow guinea boss generate
                                          heat,
      Oh boy Johnny! These streets is mean around this frolicking
                        untouchable soul.

Drafts caught in the back bang the drum slowly, only
The wedding party has Jennifer on my mind related in Spanish,
The gang that could not shoot straight made this boy's life vanish
Suspicion. Guilty by the land of cops, true confessions grow outlandish,
      Hi mom, Brazil denotes the mistress once upon a time in
                    America's fishbowl.

Born to win, the velvet iris met Stanley for desire, except
some streetcar madly dogged numerous lies called glory,
Sam kept playing that song while no ears cared to hear that story
Mission. Smother a heart given to no angel intoxicated by soporific
    oratory,
      A hundred nights and one in 1900 marked the beginning of
                    Earth with black coal.

Expectations greatly critique the monster of Shelley, though
fear has a cape tailored for a brown Jackie inconspicuously rounding
                    third base,

It is good to witness fellas hidden under a casino, another hapless paper
                                                                        chase
New York, New York! Night is the city which paints the right cheek on
                                                                    any face,
        The last tycoon was a Bronx tale fan falling in love with bloody
        mama's jackknifed mole.

A Makeshift Dream

Acute pains cleverly manipulating
silky tissue of my stomach's inner face...
a dead bird sings in winter.

The strength I dishonestly perceived in you is sinewy.
Pelting acid raindrops tap dancing on frail shoulders
every summer paralyze my incoherent mind.
I stand amongst bantam hills in a dirty city with no faith.
Swirling collages of drunken bees sucking
spiked nectar from brittle tulips
extract a naked love that doesn't pray with sincerity,
laughing with crystal tears.

I see you sitting on a sofa made of liquidated peacock feathers
and human burning flesh. The tendrils of your exterior hair
confound my subtle absorption of your deprived spirit.
A multitude of hounds howl at the ascension
of another young life laid to decomposition.
Your enameled decisions are as precious as an independent beggar.
I breathe your destitution,
Such is the touch you lay on my inner thigh like
a sunken heavy sigh bouncing to
reggae melodies and rap appetizers.

Forget the moments of misconceptualization that we never nor never
    will share...
the moon initiates an uprising of bombastic anarchy.
Please say you'll stay with a leper instead of a king, a radical instead
    of a bureaucrat, a gypsy instead of a statue, a cripple instead of a
    gymnast...
an unexpected blessing filled with pragmatic affection.

Your selection should be me.
Your selection is me.
It's obvious to everything.
Sentiments taste nugatory.

I know I could not love you.

Your presence makes me feel like I've overdosed on aspirin
and weed. If we rush into our womb at the end of our misguided
destination, we'll never reach our makeshift dreams.

You feel confused.
I do too.
The world is not alone without us.
We dictate our destinies
like Joseph Stalin making Siberia
a carousel of frozen carnivores.

There is no time to think anymore,
love is lost forever.

An Aztec warrior dances with
an African citizen of Sierra Leone,
performing hypocritical rituals of butchery,
amidst fervor of Oriental hymns and opium harmonicas.

When something good falls upon us,
we risk a tendency to commit an act of vengeance.

Give me one chance to prove to you love exists in this
    terrifying existence known as what you and I could be.
    It doesn't cost to take care of the world, it doesn't cost anything.
No iambic pentameter could describe the subtle frailties of surviving
    dead.
    Your breasts remind me of the first and last time I sucked on
    marshmallows, dripping with ecstasy mixed in heroin.

A lick of your neck makes me feel like moving downward, and
downward, and
       downward over your body that is not a consecrated temple of
       disbelief, but the assurance that an artist resides in the universe.

Every time I touch my cat for the first absorption of dawning eyes, the faint
texture of your flesh freezes the blood flowing throughout a memory of
       erections deflated by time and space...
          equivalents of irrelevance.

Zoë

I kneel on upside-down rusty nails when I pray
　　to the cardboard landscape. Escape the wartime daydream,
become a cleistogamous Mennonite committing required apostasy
　　during these apocalyptic moments. Inside swollen rooster tails,
spongy romantic orange sea horses swim, curve, tip and dance,
　　hiccupping temporal sambas to forget life's subordinate existence.
Encomiastic ocelot, your impetuous emollient Sarandon eyes
　　may never bring intimidating peace to one man's cemetery
　　sentiments.
Incandescent meniscus, the nearsighted tomorrow
is not radical enough to destroy another flying buttress.

What are we doing and where are we going?
Reverberatory inquiries everyone's ignoring.
Right-wingers exploit, liberals never stop whining,
only my tranquilized struggle lacks defining.
I'm not revolutionarily trapped in the middle,
don't give a shit about money...
of the three answers to the nebbish riddle,
it is that which is most funny...
Sometime, something, somewhere,
was not the deficiency of love
understood by Baudelaire?

Zodiac marbles plunder over awaited drumsticks of
　　haunted jubilation, my coprophilous spirit is the epitome of private
　　segregation.
What would it float like to listen to the militant fluttering
　　of your skittish eyelashes? Such indescribable refreshment,
noticing statuesque whispers taunt terrorized yellow-white
　butterflies set ablaze sashay secrets away. A brilliant Brazilian six-year
　　old

child searches overclouded streets, lapping poisonous meat
   avoiding death squad declension, walking alone, yourself to
   compete.

Though you are gone, departing before a fascinating acquaintance,
I can't help but wonder, would you like to witness the intense face
of ethereal Providence? Hence, I promise not to incite your instinctual
mechanisms of self-defense, unless you haven't already fenced in
your passion, creativity, loneliness, spirituality, and intelligence.
The way you smile reminds me of the first time I
inhaled opium scented incense, enlightening upliftment
out of the stagnate cycle of self-destructive complacence;
I lasso your inspirational essence with imaginary circumstance
for the brief path of resistance.

Pilgrimage

Sacrifice entices its instinct
moving through dark blue
paths, sad to ask Madame
where she flees or breathes for eternity.
A quaint stain making one insane
going over ostensible openings
past the crass mass attacks of pain;
anointment is a poignant point,
underneath the muttering
some understand dysfunctional acceptance.
Our independent star called
a raw prophet who sought repentance.

Slavocracy

We are wasting in a slavocracy!
I'm so alone I could shoot my depression.
Nobody can be trusted,
justice is served in a self-serving cafeteria
where the predominant indigent people
become prey to selfish religious meliorism.
Money is not the root of sin,
but afflictive proof that man
is not better than what he begins.
Lust is marketed to us like
narcotic snake oil distributed
by callous Western bedlamite doctors,
extracting what is left from their
growing cabinet of malpractice.
Those that generate, create, give
and need love are the same ones
we brutally judge. A caboose of
nomadic pigeons rest atop a
telephone livewire where communication
remains silent. They zoom over my
sleepwalking consciousness to tell me
I can never escape meditative punishment.
The heat is getting hotter
on the mafia talented streets every hour.
Lie to me and express you are not another curse.
For what is worse is worse than better sentiments
dispersed in the worst disguises.
None is wiser than the homeless fool
drenched in his own pool of honeyed piss.
Let us engage in an orgy of metaphysical intercourse
and intellectual rage as we carelessly scribble
another worthless page of sociopathic frustration

like Johnny Coltrane's thumbnails while he
magically wails and tells a tale of how
the end isn't ever happy for the end is never near enough.
the end is never there...
Tell me,
why shouldn't any of us care?

Shadow of Tomorrow

Black sparrow sinking…
      forevermore,
millions of millenniums disappear,
billions aren't worth the fear hiding behind
yesterday's vaulted door…Earthly scores aren't settled,
broken bikes petal reminiscing about moments my
opponents turned my heart into metal…hypocritical God looked
upon you and wondered why? shy as the sunrise she despised
what wasn't seen in the reflection of her bloodshot eyes…to my
surprise I was able to penetrate the lies of creation…from celestial
germination into a loving child less wild then adolescence,
presence of divinity within me…I lost when I learned in
public school the human value of being stingy—
I learned to lie
  learned to steal
  learned to cheat
  learned to hate

Didn't learn the feeling of heartbeat
lay beneath our nihilistic faith.

Enigma

High like D'Angelo
harmonizing instruments
Heaven was made for us
but never to endure
So pure
does the reflection
of your apparition
define
infinite divine cherubim
The rim is the pinnacle
of cyclical sickness
entrenched in madness
of feeling okay
Every day says
we stay together
Forever is too
dreary
weary
of fear
for nearness
of your body
turns hot into heat
and the beat
of my heart
is felt in
enigmatic
clashes.

Process of Creation

Music is the device of Satan
        lamenting the pain
        of ostracized care
        as a duet of erogenous angels
        cry for each other's company
Perversely a sole utterance
        of silence beckons
        Pandemonium
        given the circumstance
        under such an
        unforgiving conception
Never has your tongue
        worked magic like
        the shrill shriek
        of a kitten having
        its torso crippled
        by the wrath of a palm
Since the creation process failed
        humans are obliged
        to create what creativity
        will permit or recommend
Do not invoke any Muse
        for free will is an abuse
        of pleasure more
        enthralling than
        celestial measure
Endeavor to discover
        grateful enjoyment
        rooted in yourself.

Dire Inhalation

Sucking on your lips is like puffing on a Bahamazoid *leno*
without a pause for breath; once you're blazed, the initial
intake hits me as if I was not familiar with your body,
the fragile texture could crumble if fingers are not put
to rigid use with gentle precaution. A rouge glow
stimulates flames controlled by my steady pace
of mouthful movements, aromatic attacks are
not as bad as I originally fancied; forgive me
if I take all of you at once. Light-headed,
faint, progress equals your orgasmic
disappearance halfway to fatal
rapture, capture it with a
moist lick before it's all
gone. Cough! Choke!
swallowed a greedy
portion to quick;
nearer to the ass
more intensified
is the lift, shift
a little bit, the
squeeze needs
to be tighter
Where's my
lighter?

Spiritual Displacement

Centipedes…
yellow-brown…
tap dance in millions
along my
fuzzy inner thighs;

not enough tears in the overcast atmosphere
to quench the dusty Earth's unbearable thirst.

Why must we keep playing this
demented game
to see
who
comes in first?

At the bottom end
of the
universe's ulcer,
unborn aborted babies
viciously
strum painful harps
and
scream no more.

Lynx-Eyed

dirty bacterial infested water
      invested in imperialistic stolen lands
           to hydrate the poverty-stricken
                saints wasting away without
                    prophetic warning.

                        Some deliver blessings meant
                            to curse the rest.

      Worthless business negotiations top
      the elitist list of esoteric boardroom
meetings to ruin native cultures
while imposing a ubiquitous sacrilegious
      Christian monetary sepulcher in the
      middle of your crumbling pagoda.

Travel throughout nuclear shadows—
Dance with pesticide ridden locusts
weaving marred meadows—
              keep truth hidden
              fever rushes
                  first date blushes,
              hushes of nonsense
                  condense
              dense fear.
              Rainforests retard,
                lard
              swarming throughout
                your
              overweight lukewarm belly...
              it's starting to smell
                  stank.

What does a temporal decline in your over-valued stock mean to
        lean children meandering majestic
        panoramic landfills?

Abduction
of independent
thought.
Everyone
is bought.
Everything
must be
taught
about
the
lie.

                        Do not
                        submit
                        to what
                        you are
                        told.
                        Look
                        beyond
                        the mid-
                        section
                        of the
                        imperfect
                        fold to mold a deflection of sub-particle
perfection.

Elections are for corrupt disciples of Satan
                following,
                        flowing,
                                wallowing in the
                                        swallowing of steadfast nothing.

To My Mother & Father

I reluctantly saunter through eternal darkness,
my mutilated soul has no apologies
for a neglected pigeon rummaging leftover crumbs.
I cry ferociously for the forgetful moments we'll never share.
The damp aroma of charbroiled flesh smells heavier
than fox tales vaingloriously wrapped around frigid necks
of aristocratic wives. Dispersion of my disoriented version;
the virgin sunset melts like freshly scooped ice sherbert
during summer afternoon reflections.
Soon we'll be apart forever.
The gamble of life is the reward of misconception.

Timelessness

All will be redeemed.
       Faith is found in the coolness of the night sky,
       have you ever noticed how close the comatose stars are?
          Mystic chants of the aboriginal child stranded in
          a restless deciduous forest sound similar to Moonlight
                           Sonata's
       tender melancholy.
Rockets shiver,
       bullets parade, landmines erupt, bombs skydive,
       the corrupt soon discover—an eye for an eye—no one is alive.

Caressing spring showers allow crickets to frolic in shadows
dancing sundial rituals melt the poverty of Latin America's
wasteful landfills where Mayan and Incan ancestral posterity
play catch with rubber tire threaded wires from shredded tread
showing Kierkegaard and the Western mind that there is no dread.
Polar caps melt, the summer temperature scorches increase,
peace will forever play hide and seek as long as woman, workers
and indigenous everywhere never share a piece of that fertile land
given to us with an unconditional trust…

             …to drill for oil is to turn water into dust…

For who shall come in first
when we perish from hunger and thirst?
Will the worst befall the terrified selfish arrogance
of bashful survivors witnessing aftermath seclusion
from nuclear holocaust collective bargaining?
Scientific liability constructing concrete hearted laboratories lying about
cures for AIDS and cancer when all we see are mechanical treatments
treating the radiated body with naked shame, the indecipherable names
of prescribed sedating drugs;

the only effective remedy needed is a hugging kissed
touch from one loved.
When injustice and tragedy invade your household you soon decide that
life is not a game.
Bloodshot hopefulness sails interconnected canals, infected
bloodstream causing vanished dreams of paradise suppressed when
reality awakens the nightmare: spiritual
poverty.
Consecrated crystal rock, holy sagebrush whiff like harvested
strawberries
steadfast prayers arising from Labor Day ashes…windmill energy creates
heartfelt
poetry.
Harm will come to those that wield a gun but run my child to
the edge of humanity asking for a crumb of bread and a lap of wine,
soon we'll see the price of
divinity.

The Meaning of Holiness

I've never witnessed
someone so expressively beautiful
as the hurricanes that captivate your concern.

To learn from one so wise
as the nocturnal owl
is a treasure
untarnished.

The love you unequivocally give will never diminish.

When you volunteered to
comfort my distress,
I understood for the first time
the meaning of holiness.

I could lose myself
in your sorrow
forever.

Unfortunately,
the desert is much longer.

To traverse celestial
dreams is a hopeless
endeavor unmitigated;

God's love remains abated.

Surely you can tell
I'd die to adore you.

End of hours upon us,
Ravished Earth roars decrepitude,

someday the sun shall dance with the moon.

Sacred as St. Francis, audacious like erotic Theresa,
the burden of love you long to purge
is welcome forth in my permanent gloom.

Heaven By Default

An anonymous matchmaking foe as friend
May pretend to cure a trifling fancy;
'Tis this unexpected moment of death
that permanently keeps me ancy.

Two days till today I shall meet the one woman
To love, but not for marriage;
Her frightful consumption of physical thought,
My delightful neurosis she won't disparage.

Trust a fool who's an expert in love,
Trust no school with hosannas from above,
One white dove is all it takes to spread a lie;
Now do you see why?

Live life to see what happens,
Live life to be adored,
Live life to the rottenest fullest
In order to feel eternally bored.

I've seem to have forgotten, the purpose
Of such a misbegotten excursion;
Could it be that I'm the perennial stranger
Still searching for that celestial virgin?

An anonymous matchmaking foe as friend
May pretend to cure a trifling fancy;
'Tis this unexpected moment of death
that permanently keeps me ancy.

All that was discovered was a disappointment,
An anointment without olive oil;
One shouldn't give a damn to meet appointments
Predestined with amorous toil.

Our initial acquaintance was quaint,
Tainted with curtsies and false claims.
The second lacked that vivid paint
To want to remember her name.

Pints of special brewed liquor to exchange,
Greek cuisine to go Dutch;
On every date I attend, I intend
To spend not much.
Her soul dispatched a longing,
A cry I chose not to hear.
My compassion remained distant,
Far enough to be near.

An anonymous matchmaking foe as friend
May pretend to cure a trifling fancy;
'Tis this unexpected moment of death
that permanently keeps me ancy.

Such is the narrative that lacks a hero to reveal,
Fornication is all I covet, sex I couldn't steal,
Her body was the dribbling flat tire I wouldn't fix—
Her spirit possessed more magic than a silly rabbit with Trix.

Like a whistle without breath,
Sun without shade,
Every second we've spent is
Not meant to be made.

Do not forgive me,
For there's nothing to forgive;
How can one be sorry
For nothing that they did?

Time was on our side because
Time we did not share,
Invisible memories is all we have
To cherish and compare.

An anonymous matchmaking foe as friend
May pretend to cure a trifling fancy;
'Tis this unexpected moment of death
that permanently keeps me ancy.

Some People

Some people are condemned to be alone
Some are forced to permanently leave their home
Some people archive their tears for posterity
Some survive and ignore the self-righteous virtue of charity
Some folks pray to god and receive nothing
Some folks play with a dog and enjoy everything
Some individuals are lost
Some act like they're the boss
Some people never find themselves
          never find what they forgot they was looking for
people are whores, selfish, rude, inconsiderate, and cold
everyone at some time or another continues to do what they are told
Some people never grow old.

Yes

Yes—we were born into this world to be oppressed.

yes—impressed by the numerous misconceptions of success.

Yes—I detest those that claim to be the best,

yes—blessings of happiness only achieved by wanting less.

Yes—instead of aspiring to the middle echelons of the upper class,

yes—I be accumulating subversive consciousness to one day kick their ass.

Yes—conform & obey, deceive & mislead, receiving pre-conceived information from a
    business elite living for greed.

yes—must the Earth continue to spin with a barbiturate grin?

Yes—understand you have to lose in order to win.

yes—insubordinate force, remaining on an underground course to overcome a sell-out's
    remorse.

Yes—are you gonna be the one to sacrifice your soul?

yes—is integrity more important than chains of gold?

Yes—have you read Noam Chomsky's latest novel of political intrigue?

yes—is the international community under siege?

Yes—can you see the spirit dancing in the shadow?

yes—do you know why the rivers run shallow?

Yes—do you care about Third World children dying of malnutrition?

Yes—are you sincere when you recite the Act of Contrition?

Yes—are you willing to listen?

Blake

I summon darkness
like independent alchemy...
black magic Buddhists kiss a shadow,
visualizing your shocked aura stranded in naked paralysis.

If allowed to seduce you once,
I'd watch silently, meditate on the rapture of an
early grave, entice desire with malicious innocence,
disappoint with catastrophic ecstasy.

The world can have its arrogance and indifference.
Savage barbaric habitats rotten from unforgiving sympathy;
I exist in this hole talking to myself thinking I'm someone else
slowly demoralizing my mental health for the sacrament of indentured
    wealth.

The Perils of Abstinence

Microscopic beetle tentacles
riveting down my stinky sticky ass crack,
the day is sweet
when the melancholy monsoon
doesn't want to enter indoors.
Swashbuckling footsteps
titter hitherto on top
above hair stacks,
aflame the blitzkrieg
washing frosty windows.

I miss the whimper
of soft flesh.

Strange Karma

Horse hooves of death's warrant
Pursue, fucking has been tormenting fun...
Preprandial stroke of the depressed sun
Prepossesses, no more now there'll be none.
Listen...Charlie Mingus' regicidal horn seduce neglected clitoris;
Ignore this homicidal wish list of suicidal teardrops massaging ageless
    porn star fantasies Transforming into irreparable thunder clouds
    romping through night's abused transsexual Abortion; it is all
    confusion the illusion of strangled penis injecting ejaculated anxiety.
Witness smitten riggish magician continue pointless
Encounters towards evaporating rainbow, lost in light;
Embracing involuntary mortal plight is more important.
Intellectual genius handcuffed circular solitude
Gravitating around immense elm tree tops changing colors according to
    autumn's
Totalitarian flesh, dense wickedness occupied within conceptual
    pretense senses Someone must confess.
Disgusting...nothing's innocent...
Everything haunting herb smoke condensing flashes leatherback whips
    tackling
Tantrums, tantric touches screaming penetrating needle pain moaning
    freedom Burdensome strokes infantile looks telling sentimental
    jokes—abandoned from Beginning. Menacing ghost shadows
    maneuver bile flinging between slashed throats Echoing missing
    kidnapped children playing pretend around midnight cesspools,
Foozle cool. Swinging green drool infected eyelid covetous lips
    shimmering nervous
Twitches lighting arsonist matches below carbuncle parachuting dimpled
    necrosis;
Deflower powerful impulsive forcing house obstreperous bauble
    murderous naze—

Zoetic bigot...exhibitionist zombie...zetetic fetish squalid extravagant
     embrace—
Face the truth,
Cruelty is proof,
Youth adieu,
Who are You?
Life is will,
All are ill,
Age with care,
Do you dare?
Unfair world,
Past unfurled,
Future exposed,
No one knows!
If I was you,
I'd leave me alone.

Juniper Eyes

She sees the world through juniper eyes,
      tattered English imperialistic language
born infinite.

Explicit impulsive detachment,
recuperating divorcee;
lost in the shallow hills of Santa Fe.

Her robust acquiescence, languid morning mist
      infiltrating heaven dominions of demons
      admonishing tropical fern foliage
deciduous path followed for extinguished yesterday.

Her juniper eyes,
      bright blue
         egalitarian green
            everything seen
               albeit the transatlantic sheen
                  in turbulent ocean's shipwrecked dreams…
Juniper eyes, she
wishful swashbuckling
optimistic impossibility—
intellectual rebel determined, she
uprising beyond misogynistic war machine.

      my only friend, head trip random depression
      it wasn't i that made you this way, traumatized,
      stigmatized, surprised by the awkward joy unsure
      how to appreciate someone great. it's too late.
      i'd tell you to wait but let's not forget, it's the
      experience we never had that we regret.
      i wish to heal your triumphant sorrow,

tomorrow's weather foreshadows pain;
a pair of psychotics living in vain,
suicide is an answer for lovers betrayed,
we never made a promise to see the next day.

Our time spontaneous,
Sporadic like nomadic
Angels;
Gather your tears with a dandelion's feather,
Save them for the next disappointment better.

She cries on top of sun mountain
with Juniper Eyes,
despised by God for all of time.

Cries with the cougar
unable to locate her
aborted child, primal
habitat destroyed, desperate
like the unemployed.

Nervous decision to get involved.
All our problems we'll never solve.

A life lived is a life unresolved.

I hurt.
Tormented more than you can imagine,
blinded by denial.

Through beautiful Juniper Eyes,
sea breeze blue,
marijuana green,
little child molested by biological father, accosted brittle innocence
blue like sky surrounding a bright white cloud,
screaming loud, tortured enough we choose not to hear;
green like emerald taken from hard-working Amazonian
hands, pregnant at sixteen, stolen adolescence.
swimming pool blue,
Caribbean sea green,
dehydrated opulent fever rising endlessly.

Writing is a fancy rife with unfortunate hospitality
casualty of my personal war
        with Caucasian personalities
submerged between soluble words
        antagonism hidden under urban city sewers
skewed mythology
        intransigent visualizations
community owned privatization
no one cares about dismal northern England...

twice the tyranny of tomorrow's woes.

In debt we dance hypnotically wishing for
cocaine to hinder the onslaught of expectant ochlocracy.

In debt to unseen idiots on the east coast somewhere in Delaware,
spendthrift addict traveling our imagination for the time being.
Hating our jobs we seek to improve life through fantasy.

The world is a clever aphorism for nothingness.
You are not a highness, but a benevolent elephant,
longtime staring at the malevolent ground;
reality is too much for my dislocated parentheses.

The weakness inside your skin languishes with ruling class desire.
Hair uncombed, dirt makeover, disturbed embrace, frittering
        punch hole madness around skyscraper memories.
Smooth wrinkled flesh encapsulated nightmare,
polygamist memorandum,
soothing moan, bemoaned departure.

I've launched the hidden, excruciating taught stomach gargling like a
cauldron boiling infidels worshipping shit stains barbaric white images
translucent sex marathon soaked sheets in sweat and red cum; middle
finger smells like recently burned marble candle wax.

She—destitute cute covered in second-hand Virginia's Secret stash sauntering around a rickety hovel rented by acquisitive newcomers not knowing how to operate a syndicate of slumlord atonement.

I found her—She—exhibiting loneliness, soft purple liquid gushing out her lacerated eyelid, the vanity punishing medium-sized rodent wandering around her matted oily hair and the maggots breathing beneath her four week old child crawling out of her ripped womb growing gray wings with feathers falling off slowly; sentenced to death twice before birth, hounded by societal infatuations, imprisoned half-breed boyfriend found shaking naked dripping narcolepsy, disdainful sunlight, burned skin tags, scarred permanence.

She—your sickness makes me succumb, my soul sold on the black market.
In my indifference I perceive received epiphanies.

> The truth of your insecurities, unresolved issues of men persecuting, no promiscuity left inside your untouched lust

> I miss your philanthropic touch...

Juniper Eyes,
> spring pasture green,
>> light hazel plea,
>>> tumultuous soul serene.

Where was your kindliness when you unleashed the butcher knife's arrogant shimmer? Frightened like the last time I died.
I darted for the front door—you rammed the metal into my head,
condemned and damned my holiness lost easily
in a loosely organized insurrection.
We epitomized illogical perfection.

The flashing lightning illuminates your stern,
strenuous face clenching jaws and fists.

I punish you with manic thrust after panic trust,
your soiled pubic hairs brushing mine dry.

Peter Gabriel is composing agony on the radio,

I remember in high school I used to wish
desperately for a woman I noticed to notice me
and now I see the worthlessness of desire
as my warm heart develops worms of fire
tunneling through my suffocating arteries,

I've never had a companion…and now it's time to leave.

The Fortunate Misfit Who Counts Blessings

The last time she cried
was when her padrastro kicked her
in the belly for being 7 months pregnant at 17.
7 years later he perished
and her stomach felt warm and nervously calm.
When her child turned 7
she accidentally misplaced the juvenile
somewhere in the midland barrios
of the Holy Faith City.
The only cross she lost
was the monthly welfare benefit.
Since then, 7 times
the state hospital has been a place of convalescence.
No blood relations,
homeless shelters,
abandoned structures,
dry arroyos,
or 7-11s would open their embrace.

Frozen intimations of retrospect
conjure shrill glares of silence.

7 deadly sins and only one way to commit them.

It is not that she doesn't care anymore about the world,
beggars and solicitors of proprietary love
always occupy a den of bloodshot radiance.
Her 7 venereal dependents continuously and rapidly
guarantee a better existence
while she focuses on the ground.

Ephemeral

You are a tragedy—
wicked orchid dying prematurely,
before I could appreciate your beauty.

Skeletal Remains

You are a curse I covet.
I want to love you but I'll never admit it
to myself or anyone else: You are poison for my mental health.
You don't want an intellectual nor one who will drive you mad on the
    sexual tip...
you want someone whose going to treat you like shit.
You desire emotional pain,
enjoy dirty rain,
you refrain from trying to love again;
you could care less about what you could gain from a gentle soul
whose only goal is to provide a cushion when you fall;
you are a small woman trying to stand tall in a desperate world of
    unfulfilled dreams,
you are the end that doesn't justify the means.

Nameless

Nameless.

Your name remains within my vanishing memory
as beautiful as innocent incense smoke,
recklessly mimicking a drunken flamenco dancer under a
hallucinating candlewick's ruthless ulster shine.

In the restless thick of the urban meadow's thankless weeds,
Inescapably ensconced in society's ruinous
Irresponsible censorship; I search
For eternal loneliness...bliss...in the off hand
Chance I shall regretfully reap what I wish.

The sunlight's a puppet master, burning out
My ruined retinas, speaking with soft insurrectionary whispers
when I suddenly notice you're not as bashful as you used to be,
Desperately maimed by unjustifiable hierarchy.

If survival is your motive you shall fail
In your temporary fruitless operations;

It takes one experience of a stranger
To understand the hostile definition
of remorseless premonition.

Nameless.

In the restless thick of the urban meadow's thankless weeds,
Inescapably ensconced in society's ruinous
Irresponsible censorship, your name remains
Within my vanishing memory
As beautiful as innocent incense smoke,

Recklessly mimicking a drunken flamenco dancer
Under a hallucinating candlewick's ruthless ulster shine.

Some day I shall lie to my grandchildren and say you were almost mine.
But until that moment never arrives, I shall lie to myself and feverishly
    imagine
You and I endlessly lost, oppressed by the universe's untrustworthy
    intendance of time.

Calm

I remember the fist time I made her cry.

It was because I made a fatal error
worthy of ignorance.
She listens to cracks in jagged glass,
endlessly hoping to feel the significance
of a broken promise.

All I do is think of her...
the day's activities for an
indispensable slave seem far away.

The trepidation of an insect about to be smashed
infects my contorted libido, pontificating truth
to roadblocks of simpletons telling us what to do.
If the instance appeared to where I licked her melting flesh
with a fresh inconspicuous gesture of loyal degradation,
yesterday's mess would be left where it rests.
Bad timing, desperate calm hating the self more than the other.
Frivolous nightmare, uncontrollable sleep, deep sentiments trapped
in an overheated exploding heart. Desirous winter fling, eternal nothing,
    bedside
tantalizing dream, intense nocturnal submission died faster than a rite of
    spring.
Her disappointed enchantment with me is liquid blessing induced
    indiscriminately.
What a fool I've become,
witnessing the first time a robin rescue her young,
escorting the dying thing back to the nest to convalesce.
Distressed. Defeated. Torn. Worn out. Weary.
Am I not too strong to sustain
the lovely pain she inflicts every time she directs

her fractured index finger toward this lingering flame?
Her tormented disposition is a welcomed imposition,
composition of Chopin's disorderly meter and
Debussy's flowery-keyed artillery. A panoramic centipede,
scuttling not a millimeter in case we make her bleed without touching.

Fate has caught up with me.
She is to me what subtlety is to beauty,
lunacy to heresy.

I remember the last time I made her smile,

kissing wistfully at the airport gated community,
blushing like someone who's afraid of simplicity.

Something Beautiful

Life is a struggle fought in vain,
death is but a wish away.

I thought I spotted her plane
flying over the Santa Fe nighttime serenade,
but when the jet stream emitted its final mist,
I noticed instead the brightness of her permanence.

Life is a battle lost in pain,
death is but a wish away.

The exasperating vision of her slender nakedness
rising through morning freshness like a tulip
unfolding its breath, makes me regret every second I slept.
A secret that must be kept.
The depth of her loneliness
is equivalent to the redemptive
quality of my wretchedness.

We hold hands like we've imagined we've done it before,
she sings rushed soliloquies in hushed reminiscence,

possibility is nonsense for the non-believer,
I do my utmost worst not to deceive her,
and still I can't perceive how she can receive
my ignominious desire without a trace of resistance.

Life is a distance that cannot be attained.
Death is only an insignificant game
acknowledged by no other name.

The Requiem

he wanted to but @ the
mean it but
end didn't

...And all I ever wanted to do
      was to mean what I say when I said I love you...

I think I'm dying,
      trapped in a black heart compartment torn apart from the start;
      handing you my soul for free.   *I did this*

Something simple as love is not easy—
      food for the homeless,
      wine for the sober,
      addict of thought, emotion, and misery.
You are a sorceress,
      scandalous as honest intentions soaked in a cauldron of ritual
      hypocrisy.

The habitual games we play,
fustian words we say,
almost make me run away...yet and still I stay...wasting carelessly every
      day.

I had a nervous breakdown for the first time,
      before I became your sideshow gimcrack;
Lacking independence, pretense, and a place to call my own.
Little world of delusional hope, alone in tranquility,
flown across the universe to find destiny at home.

...And if I offered you cosmic bliss you wouldn't believe it, for that
would be impossibly true...And if I wrote you a poetic masterpiece
you wouldn't remember it, because you'd know it wasn't written for
you...And if I said I wanted to make desperate love to you you wouldn't
accept it...anyways...I have know idea what to do...And if masturbation,
narcissistic murder, and staring forever at the breathing blank walls is all

I have for physical expression, spiritual depression, then it will be written in history books nobody reads, I had to learn my lesson.

Karma has given me chance after chance, one blessing after the other, I've shunned her grace, laughed in her generous face,
all I ever wanted was a friend I call lover.

But now it's over, for here you are, I feel your power without your presence, hanging on a string, listening to birds sing every tortuous morning, wishing I could sleep in your ignorance, capitulating to my wayward dreams of holding you endlessly, obsessed with the last time we kissed under a falling tree, crying for your understanding and awareness, beware of life's only last lonely mystery—
love's lost liberty.

The Beautiful Distraction

My attraction to her is intense
like the bloodthirsty white man's
warlord desire for instantaneous death.

Her praying mantis neck,
is flesh of regret,
lest we forget...
that and only that
is what I covet.

Nevertheless,
blessed is this ransacked consciousness
subdued by wasted hours facing meaninglessness,
pettiness prophetic pretty fabulous seamstress
rummaging around an aversive soul.

To kiss her is to taste the final breath.

My masterpiece is more important,
more potent than a shoddy service of maleficence,
the bloodstains hemorrhaging ferociously
inside my cardiovascular magnificence cannot
endure any longer her anxious elixir,
returning once again to deprive me
of deceitful sleepiness.

With shameful hands, bashful arms wrapped tightly ensconced
between her hermetic loneliness, sun ascension daydreams, smiling
demons haunt me displaying tortured rumpled photographs of stripped
Lebanese children showering shamelessly beneath omnivorous
overcast cascading downpours of metallic clamped clusters exploding
indiscriminately slicing intestines still digesting loss of innocence.

Hold me forever near the uproarious hysteria beneath her sepulchral breasts.

Under shredded blankets, bathing in scorched obscurity, she closes her dreamless persistence like pestilence unsure of where to fly. Eyes half-closed sit statuesque upon her weariness, sauntering around what is left. Fathomless unmistakable dreariness penetrates uncompromising desire lashing out incommensurable wantonness seducing only with scanty reminiscences of liquid putrescence.

Find me lying nuptial beside her inflammatory stillness,
Fondle my penis with shadow magic ancient trance wisdom,
Fecundity to solitary confinement bare breasted alongside
her restless promiscuity.
She cares to be cuddled in conflagrant nostalgia.
The flamboyant moon radiates
midnight wayward sentinels practicing
slippery orgies of mass engrossment.

She yearns to thrust my dissolute passion readily down her scanty throat in order to sanctify what is left of our dwindling relationship. She burns between ignored weeping flesh, swishes daintily every time I shove my fingertips into her antiquated world.

She dances like an uneducated schoolgirl.

Talented miscreant,
lamenting bashfully,
post-suicidal catastrophe
undulating slanted figuratively,
seek this inappropriate opportunity
to challenge futile limitations of her unlimited opiate.

Stare at me like we're starving,
Lunge at me with cuticle companionship,
Smother me in solitude.

Fragrant mornings seem somber
surrounding her incongruous formation;
The decompressed waist,
The shanty saccharine tresses which switch color frequently because
    she's strange,
The impure pussy that soaks the brain in permanent suspension,
The whimsical playfulness of her unsophisticated artistry,
The pain she causes me.

I plot to desecrate the great totems,
to deconstruct the grandiose 21st Century arsenals.
I conspire to punish the wealthy with tortuous instruments
devised by the working poor utilizing
the garrison palisade.

No matter how much she lies to me with every inscrutable concoction
of calculated flattery, physical beauty distracts me from acknowledging
the internal foundation of her pre-meditated usury.

She is straightforward,
informs me of truth revealed to her
during a duration of delicate hostility.

I love it when we talk of death,
like there's no consequence to frivolous decadence.
She pretends she is in love with me for the past dispensation,
pretends she is enthralled beyond ordinary belief
at the sight of my unlikely resurrection,

I attempt to cheat her infatuation.

Just when I begin to devise and manipulate my genius…
        she possesses thighs of a pompous albino flamingo
        falling inquisitively asleep at the sight of unseen,
        to the sound of whispering feet, trembling every groan
immersed in mutual
        obsession with wholesome perversion.

Just when I commence a spiritual sentence...
        sacrificial uncontrollable lustful ritual captivates her inattention
        to the pulsating arteries fast with mildewed contradiction;
        drip to evaporation
        sweat to silence
        hush to stillness
        the swap between juvenile fantasies.
And just when the world's about to end...
        she pretends she's in love with me, the forsaken human
        suffering for nothing. My generous contagion
        is her unhealthy preoccupation with me;
        only she can bewitch the numinous progeny within.

Dear Anonymous

I feel like a 5th grader again, reluctantly participating in my first spring dance, self-consciously gawking across the roily gym floor, hoping one of the sweet scenting young ladies three-quarters of a world away shall saunter my direction and present her hand to silently signify that a liberating tango has been politely requested. This is how I am every time I see you. On my dreadful journey towards the exit, I bashfully glance upwards to the left, telepathically call out your being to notice me, and if you do, just for one snap or two, quicker than the jungle prance of a camouflaged jaguar on it's meditative prey, I lower my stubbly chin averting my fleeting eyes in order not to recognize your expressionless countenance.

The corrupting vision of your flashing image is too mysterious. I don't know what to do. It seems as if your talismanic vibes shield your cherished space and ward off the pervading evil that is the male ego. During other hallucinatory dimensions, more than thrice I've apprehended you stealing a cautious glimpse aimed at my demure aura. The memory remains awkward. Perhaps I just want to meet your acquaintance so bad that I foolishly convince myself you are looking at me. I don't want to make you uncomfortable. I only continue to peek your way because I sense your strong presence like an Appaloosa sniff's the atmosphere's trepidation before it begins to rain, recklessly searching for a dilapidated stable's shelter in consternation of relishing dampness.

I desire nothing except an early death. I covet love only to encounter her oppression. What I want from you has nothing to do with why the persistent moon groans every autumnal night in all it's heavy brightness for another fruitless harvest. I would listen to your justified universal grievances without lust. If you ever needed the closest thing to a human friend, perhaps I could pretend to be the one you'd pretend to trust. Disgusted by my lack of giving, I've been thriving behind the masquerade of iniquity. Maybe you could teach me how to be holy. I have no clue of who you are or what you can be. It's curiosity's envy.

Therefore it makes it easy for me to honestly lie as the deceiving truth touches your lamenting spirit gently. I hope to flirtatiously exchange 'hellos' and 'good-byes' before the decomposing Earth's final battle cry. Sometime when the future's near, I will whisper into your wax laden ear and abolish your worshipping fears of not knowing where you're going, not knowing where you stand, not knowing that I know you already got a man because merciless, pernicious experience has repetitiously taught me that women as obviously attractive as you are, usually drag around throughout the barren ground a ton weighted chain of misogynistic pain in the form of some swinging dick schmuck that just wants to fuck, driving you in his new flashy car...continuously polluting the air we inhale with every puff from the exhaust pipe due to every push of the pedal due to the heavy metal parading bullets penetrating youthful lives brainwashed by the lies known as "freedom" and elitist national security.

Allow me to pursue the beauty that patiently waits beneath your resplendent skin, the beauty I witnessed once through the channel of your untrammeled grin.

Nothing

Lost in this soulless world, human beings seem more like demonic fiends without a religious mission. I admire nothing about no one. People are like unexpected hives ignorantly emerging on your neglected flesh after you've brushed a subtle leaf of basil on purpose. If one human being had to stand out in my memory as someone less than admirable but more than malodorous, it would have to be a certain closed book named Angelo. I slaved with him at an illegal prison camp for plant life, cleaning chemicals I never heard of and rat shit from storage space unkempt throughout the past therefore it wasn't my mistake, it wasn't my responsibility to do the bidding of formidable stupidity manifested in the entertaining form of God's little retarded imperfections. Angelo was like a snowflake that didn't belong in the overcrowded sky; falling from nowhere, beautiful like an innocent lapse in the storm's calming aggression, isolating him into my life before he died out and disappeared as snow drifts to evaporating dust. He was one of the most significant figures in my cheap existence because I never got to know him intricately. He forever remains a decomposing dream. I took his workplace palaver for granted and mistook it for sociopathic withdrawal instead of for what it really was; companionship sacred. Through his inoculating eyes, his intense rhetoric, I summoned hadean spirits to help me begin to comprehend the magic I was blessed with since birth. He enabled me to govern the direction of my powers. Within his presence I soared to the inner sanctum of the sun. Atrocity made sense, injustice was justified, and the infinite weaknesses of the failing human experiment were forgiven. He didn't speak of heaven, he knew of somewhere better. I would mention consciousness but that's just a cliché for the banausic chic. It was much more than societal sanctioned infatuation. He exposed intelligence for all its profanity. He located the truth for seconds at a time and taught me that a lie is only a lie if you lie to those that lie. I began to question the pseudo self-appointed so-called authority of my state instituted instructors and the administrators, bureaucrats, and sinister politicians that control them.

My boss at my meaningless job no longer remained my boss. I saw and see the world as egalitarian with me nowhere in it. I fell in love with Buddha, cursed Jehovah, embraced Satan as a brother, satirized Marx and repudiated all of them accordingly when the time never arrived. This quintessential turned me on to Hubert Selby Jr, Carlos Castaneda, John-Paul Sartre and a host of incurable fevers. I fell in love with his ideas, not his decaying carnal incarnation. I learned to listen and learned to love learning. He talked to me once sincerely. After that I put away the cocaine and understood how to confront my fear and pain alone and lonely. I used to look at him from afar when he thought I thought he wasn't looking, knowing he would cradle my incorrigible whereabouts. I wish I could understand his sorrow and promise him happier tomorrows.

The Valentine

For Valentine's Day
I gave my love an abortion.

Never have I shed so many tears
for one woman.

She smiles occasionally
when the mesmerizing winter sun
sets ablaze impatiently,
waiting desperately for spring.

Together we sing hymns of depression;
The aggression of our lust left us
nothing but sorrowful lovemaking sessions,
wasted time to learn a difficult lesson.

I offered her a promise
saturated with emptiness,
wish fulfillment fantasy,
weariness and demented dreams…

Every time we touch is only a taste of what it seems.

Her powerful incarnation left me bewitched
like staring at a photograph of someone dead…
Her soft sifting skin provides a masticating cushion,
Blood that spills leaves everything unsaid.

Inside her soul I thought was lost
rests a child that can never be born…
Inside her heart I thought was not,
wanders a spirit from midnight until morn.

Trapped inside a tiny claustrophobic cove,
lying naked in a bed made for one body,
we chant misleading proclamations of love;
the decisions we make,
the life we take,
is something enough
to never again speak of.

For Valentine's Day
I gave my love an abortion...

a whimsical portion
of cynical distortion
to display my debilitated affection;
the opportunity elapsed,
destiny collapsed,
we live a death of indiscretion.

I remember the precise moment we conceived...
amidst palindromic baths of blood,
inside a warm sticky atmosphere,
the fear I once possessed
condensed my sickly apprehension
to release my sterile quintessence
into her immaculate ovulating presence.

For Valentine's Day
I did not give my love
the gift that is superficial,
our relationship is special:
        she did not receive used bouquets of wilting roses,
        nor bottles of bargain wine,
        she did not receive crumpled boxes of poisonous chocolate
        nor something less divine.
                I couldn't afford Paris
                though I know she's been there before,
                I couldn't afford a hotel room

with a privately enclosed door.
We held each other close as if nightmare
were all we knew…
knowing exactly what we had to do.
We walked along the river bed dry,
Talked about giving it a try…

We'd regret it till the day we die.

I love my love like no love I've ever known.
Strength, honesty, and belief I should've shown.
I've grown so much since that cold day in February,
A body we buried underneath a desecrated cemetery.

For Valentine's Day
I did not write my love a poem…
    I didn't waste what little money I have
    on a ceremonial expensive diamond ring…
    I didn't compose a matrimonial serenade to sing…
    I didn't take her on an extensive romantic cruise…
    I gave her something of nothing left to lose…
We can never know if
what we did was wrong;
The most important thing was to carry on.
I kept telling her how brave she was, courageous, and strong.
She's the most beautiful, tantalizing woman that walks the decomposing
    planet…
She has shimmering brown hair that falls over her glimmering face
like wild water over a mountain cliff,
She retains caliginous eyes that discern
the difference between ephemeral truth and eternal lies.
She smiles demure like a virgin's
first comprehension of forbidden trepidation;
My love is a constellation with fourteen stars
that resemble the fate of Mayan civilization;
her heart was shaped by an architect's imagination.

I love my love like no other love I'll ever see.
We did what we did in order to be free.

Our child is a beautiful spirit that looks like her mother,
talks like his father,
walks with mysteries of infinite galaxies.
Our child is a reflection of
our demented romantic fantasies.

He has his mother's incomparable genius,
Her father's beloved waywardness,
Her mother's clairvoyant calculation,
His father's inconsideration,
His mother's loving nature,
Her father's low-life stature,
Her mother's vast learning capacity,
His father's insecure tenacity,
His mother's proclivity for reckless adventure,
Her father's productivity of meaningless conjecture,
Her mother's beauty,
His father's calamity,
His mother's diverse talents,
Her father's aversion to violence,
Her mother's long sexy legs,
His father's incapacity to beg,
His mother's work ethic,
Her father's ethnocentric eccentric ethnic,
Her mother's touchable creamy skin that zaps the lips on every kiss,
His father's opportunities missed.

Our child is a magnificent child that lives
in a universe we cannot comprehend,
Our child lives in a place that never ends.

For Valentine's Day
I sat with my love

listening to Nick Drake
compose his litany of suicidal melancholy;
For Valentine's Day
I made a commitment to my love
consisting of folly and finale.

In this suspended world we are dead souls who roam...
We did what we did to give our child a home.

Swollen breasts,
        bloated stomach,
                expanding uterus.

Indeterminate constipation,
        excruciating cramps,
                drips of blood on a napkin.

I wish I could've given her something else,
I can't help but feel I ruined her health.

At the Cross of the Martyrs,
she finally decided to starve the unborn
of a life filled with insecurity,
doubt, fear, and poverty...
love is antinomy to responsibility.

I cried in her arms lying naked under
the burning afternoon sun,
lamenting over what I had done.
I've always been pro-choice
but never understood what that meant,
until we underwent a lifetime of one experience.

A scar on her uterus,
        A scar on his neck,
                A scar on their soul
                        they will never forget.

I offered her a promise
saturated with emptiness,
wish fulfillment fantasy,
weariness and demented dreams…

Every time we touch is only a taste of what it seems.

I love my love like no other love I'll ever see.
We did what we did in order to be free.

I love my love like no love I've ever known.
Strength, honesty, and belief I should've shown.
I've grown so much since that frozen day in February,
A body we buried underneath a desecrated cemetery.

For Valentine's Day
I gave my love an abortion…

Never have I shed so many tears
for one woman…
we live a death of indiscretion.

Our child is a magnificent child that lives
in a universe we cannot comprehend,
Our child lives in a place that never ends.

Book III
Emancipation

...And The Pursuit of Happiness

I'm just like all the rest...
Working hard and doing my best...
So I can make it to the top
and call it success,
only to look down on my fellow insects.

In The Workplace

In the workplace,
we have snitches,
bitches, and fuckin idiots
protecting the machine
that incarcerates us all.

Utilitarian Reassurance of Personality in Capitalist Society

Every single fuckin day I feel like shit!
Shit in da morning, shit in da afternoon,
shit in da evening. Open me up and
take a look for yourself. No one takes
care of me, neglected as if I was homeless.
Little dicks piss all over me, huge assholes spit in my face.
Bitches dispose of shit that I have trouble swallowing sometimes.
Quite often, I myself regurgitate, but it is da regurgitators who give
a salty fuck about my condition; returning home in da wee hours of da
morning from some stupid ass adventure that allowed them da privilege to
orally display what fuckin idiots do with their spare time. Of course I'm bitter.
You would be too if all your activity consisted of standing still, never blinking.
Just waiting for your asshole masters to use their assholes so they could make
an asshole out of you. Fuckin Assholes! Those are my Rembrandts, Monets.
Used, Used, Used, Used like a fuckin rubber plunger.
My shithole even smells like one.
Rust, lime, dust, scum…
these are my acquaintances.

Southpaw Go Home

The white ring conservative coalition controls
everything in Amerika!
No bullshit son, weez got it locked down like
spics and niggas.
I figure
our destiny manifested
soon as we arrested
a barren land
(from a Redman)
to expand
coast 2 coast
and boast
a kingdom some
say will pay
on
the
Day
of Judgment.

Is not everyone aware that *our* GOD gave *us* the world to do what the
    fuck *we* want,
                                then justify it?

We make wars to bring peace,
We make laws to pay for Justice's glasses,
We established morals
                values
                ethics
                etiquette
                decorum
                amenities
                civilities

and
decency.
So when I say "Behave Mothafucka": you do it.
When I say "The Amerikan Dream": you pursue it.
When I give you a governmental handout: you boo it?
So who's to say what's right or wrong,

Except ME!

Gingrich?

Newt is Christ with an anti-gay agenda—
"Praise the Lord" that <u>Bob</u> is <u>Doleful</u>;

Clinton

Bill gets slick with his willy while the nation suffers—
KOSOVO IS INTOLERABLE (but Granada was O.K.); *?*

The Storm in the Desert created a hero out of a Bush that didn't burn
but spoke the truth to the populace when thin lips couldn't be
discerned.

Instead of thinking of rebellion
you proletariats should be working,
Youz the underdog like the Italian
while I'm the German smirking.

My posterity is priority over any minority who's no authority but a frailty
and depravity of society caught up in a Disneyworld reality. Actually   *ha!*
abortion should be legal for your accidental births that aren't worth the
greasy refugees you smuggle across the holy cross that is our border.   *migrants*

it'snotthatI'mabigotfacistracist,
I'mjustuncouthdisrespectfulspitefulandtasteless.

I apologize
for those lies that promised you creatures some sort of education.
<u>Literature, Music, Art, Ballet, and Theatre are gated communities</u>
<u>for VIPs = Veritably Impudent Personifications.</u>   *luxuries*
So don't be beguiled
by upliftments

and unfulfillments
known as
rights for the civil.
The only civil being
is the hero fiend
like Milton's Satan
dominatin
my country
'tis of thee
so one day
we may all see
the forthcoming
of
nothing,
Yeah
I'm fronting!

Insubordination

I don't drive no SUV!
My heart's not filled with
Amerikan greed. No need to
bleed poor people with
archaic surgical procedures
of severe racial prejudice translated into economic gospel.

This capitalistic melting pot is killing us,
                              scorching us,
                        burning our backs,
but we lack the subversive education to eradicate private property *William Julius*
     inflation   *Wilson*
in the untied united hands of networking business elites.
The streets are waiting,
        wanting to be taken
                by hungry affinity groups of
radical tumbleweeds that can't flake when facing police confrontation.
I'm tired of state initiated repression!
I'm sick with leukemia of nuclear waste dumping recycle centers.
I have no rights granted by a constitution written
        to establish prison institutions — *schools?*
        with no hope for
        wealth redistribution
        nor hourglass retribution.
Good things come to those who wait, but great things come to those
     that fight.
Through the mysterious night the might of the patient masses shall
     welcome the warm light to kick the exposed asses of the cold
     wealthy classes, and live in fear no longer.

Killer Cop, Killer Cop, Don't Stop!

Killer Cop, Killer Cop, Please don't stop!
Drop another sloppy spic quicker than the
Other nigger you buried last night in the big city in a hurry.
One shot, two shot, three shot, nine shot ten…
Fend for your frightened programmed life killer cop
…tic-toc, tic-toc…
Killer cop,
was it your chickenhearted pop that stuffed
      his syphilitic cock up your rectal snuffbox,
          reaching around,
          tip-toe touching ground,
          no one hears the wheezy sound,
          —pound after pound after pound after pound—
          TOUCHDOWN!
Killer cop…was it?
Is that what it was that made you become the vengeful fuzz in the first
place?
Only to waste your unexamined existence chasing punk
wanna-be gangsta pranksters
      perambulating around the abandoned barrio,
      meditating to ambulance sirens screaming all night
              Oughta Sight!
Killer cop,
  don't stop there.
Whatta you care?
      All them greasy haired wetbacks attack each other anyway,
                 murdering their brother
              committing mirthful fratricide…
          cursing their mother
          unremitting birth dissatisfied…
lied to about the religious spermicide now my pride intensified trapped
inside the formaldehyde aroma dipped doublewide alongside the

county landfill dumpsite blindsided by the blue-eyed parasite residing in
a million-dollar mansion on my ancestor's hilltop
ONCE MORE.

Oh sure, sure…killer cop.
joypop another tablet of speed
and indeed we'll rid this Protestant country 'tis of thee
entirely of the indigenous immigrant seed,
the proletarian community…
Make 'em bleed killer cop—
make 'em bleed for me,
You see—
I can't lock-up dem brown sharecroppers no longer. I ain't got no room
in my overcrowded super maximum-security multi-billion dollar ever
expanding prison industry to feed these primitive, uncivilized baboons.
Soon the chicken eating coons and bean pickin goons just might get
it together at high noon, low moon, and realize that it will take much
more than a white missionary Weatherman to start the delusional
revolution. What did that hip-hop backward country rasta Negro Jeru da
Damaja say once, "Organizational skills kills more devils than bullets."
       "Organizational skills kills more devils than bullets."
Gosh, it just might happen killer cop…

…tic-toc, tic-toc…

HA!
what a sophistic joke.
I got 'em all doped up,
Socioeconomically broke,
psychologically depressed, hence
Spiritually broken! Smokin that shit,
       sucking corporate dick,
       searching for elusive tit and prude ass all through the early dawn…
There nothing but enslaved pawns that don't even belong on my
checker-passed chessboard—unless, unless, they are willingly forced to
do my world dominating,
                                            empire building,

capitalist destructive bidding best.
But none shall pass my national standardized test
of hopelessly trying to achieve materialistic success.
Killer cop, Killer cop...
Flip-flop, co-op the teenybop bebop fables of Aesop, swap your Gestapo
    flattop at your local pawnshop for a tattooed teardrop...
Killer cop, Killer cop...you myopic psychotic misanthropic motherfucker!
Drop another sweatshop candidate
        that wants to debate
        the forbidden hidden agenda issues:
Kill the undesirable refugees
that refuse to line-up for second-hand tissue—
Kill the poor killer cop, kill the poor!
More and more undesirable second-class citizens
continue to invade this contaminated denizen
of power struggling butchers called businessmen.
Killer cop, you are the protector of the ultra-wealthy
with your minimum wage earning capacity—
what woolgathering tenacity it requires to
        fire, fire, fire on the unarmed killer cop:
                plant a knife
                rape the wife
                do it twice
        and pay the price of an administrative paid vacation
        anywhere throughout this police state nation
        hosting biblical parades to cover-up our
        reciprocal political charades killer cop.
One shot, two shot, three shot, ten shot twenty...
Plenty biased judges hold cruel and unusual grudges against civilians
even though you're the death blow villain,
                    killing black and brown children,
                    dealing confiscated drugs;
                feeling-up sixteen year-old clitoris,
                begging for one more statutory hug.
Killer cop, killer cop, don't stop!
airdrop your tip-top brainwashed SWAT team on those demonized
peaceful demonstrators mobilizing against war;

Kill the poor, kill the poor!
chop off the bookshop heads of those individuals that teach humanity
    to think;
Kill the poor, kill the poor!
eavesdrop on those that organize to liberate the meek;
Kill the poor, kill the poor!
some more some more some more you myopic psychotic misanthropic
    motherfucker!

...tic-toc, tic-toc...

The Dirty Sanchez
—for Maestas, Bustamante, and Chavez

Little brown man, little brown man,
stay out of my way.
Little brown man, little brown man,
shit stains in your brain.

...you've spent your whole pathetic life sucking little dick of a brittle
gringo prick, now you're stuck in a chiseled fake norm. Little brown man
with a subtle plan to treat your brothers with scorn. For the shriveled
gringo the little brown man tells tales of riddles and fables in order to
be able to salvage his stable full of shit and sit comfortably in puddles
of rum soaked piss. He'll belittle his sister, say master or mister, and
play with second-hand vittles bestowed in a bottomless pit. Gringo is
your idol, addled recitals in a cauldron of denial, cradled vital delusions
of survival. Little brown man, little brown man, dilly dawdle or diddle.
Pluck strings on an outworn fiddle, drink mold from a rust laden kettle,
and still settle for less. Little brown man, little brown man, why should
you ever second-guess? Perhaps it's because your lips are chapped from
sucking dick and kissing gringo ass. Who's the boss when your dreams
get tossed due to a heart made out of glass? The crass white man
will meddle in your affairs without a care for your children or culture.
Little brown man, little brown man, why must you prepare dinner for
a vulture. You stand five feet tall, that is all, in world full of men where
you can't contend...you got something to prove, so do what you do,
but be prepared to crawl. You couldn't play basketball, you make love
to a midget, you wear high healed sneakers, pump bass through your
speakers, when your gringo boss calls your little body fidgets. Little little
little brown man your spittle shines loaded on his whittled penis; take
your tongue from his rectum, it's okay to disrespect them, no matter
what he thinks of himself he is not a fuckin genius. Little brown man
you are the quintessential corporate whore, little brown man, little
brown man, go on and do your favorite sell out chore. Settle the score

for gringo, shuttle immigrants from Mexico back beneath the border on a bus made of gringo order, protect the law, loosen your jaw, because gringo himself isn't much shorter. Protect his prisons from the likes of you, become a cop and shine his shoes, no matter what decision you make you will always lose. Little brown man, little brown man, even cattle act unsettled when they're about to be huddled into a hoard through a slaughterhouse gorge where the blood splats and gurgles, but you little brown man your blood never cringes nor curdles when gringo dictates before you insurmountable obstacles and hurdles.

Little brown man, little brown man,
stay out of my way.
Little brown man, little brown man,
shit stains in your brain.

Little brown man, little brown man, I'm tired of your tattle-tale mutterings of unsettled inferiority complexes showing two faces to the world...little brown man, little brown man, you'll always be nothing more than a pathetic stupid little girl.

Ode to Phudds

Phuddy duddy went to the bathroom to take a piss. When Phuddy duddy returned all the phudds had the eternal crotch itch. Phuddy duddy woulda putta rubber on its mouth, but Phuddy duddy got a phudd in chemistry. Coulda phudd move mud without gloves if a phudd putta bud on a dud? Not unless the concubine is a phudd. Phuddy duddy is a pussy cuz phudds shoulda studied humanity but phudds are Phuddy duddies only if silly puddy woulda done a good deed. Phuddy duddy shoulda been a daddy but Phuddy duddy is the dud not the dad that lost a seed like a fad, too fuckin bad. No sympathy for Phuddy duddy because Phuddy duddy shoulda been nice but a phudd is a buddy only to other Phuddy duddies since all phudds are fucked-up on their own shit. Do all Phuddy duddies wear crooked glasses and power fuckin coats over the ego? Phuddy duddy shoulda putta rubber on its mouth but phudds must've lost its accent instead of putting up with phudds outside of education. Is a phudd educated or castigated? Is a phudd castrated? Can a phudd be smarter than a fart and still be part of phudd society? Phuddy duddy went to the people to teach them something new. Little did Phuddy duddy know the people don't know no more than you.

Job

I'm trapped in a fantasy,
      country of hypocrisy;
decadence is the basis of Western Philosophy.
From the Socratic Method, Machiavelli
to Existentialism;
      The 21st Century is the age of deconstructive capitalist
imperialism.
        Stolen resources, incinerated tropical rainforests,
        genocidal global warming is not enough of a warning.
        Sub-Saharan Sudanese ethnic cleansing? *Darfur*
        Is that a euphemism to be politically correct
        or is it a reality check?
Al Qaeda is still on the payroll of Bush Sr.
Because of his Anglo-Saxon cold sterile demeanor,
he gets away with mass larceny and murder while I spend months
behind bars for a petty misdemeanor.
        There's no justice in a corrupt society!
Idiotic intellectual inferiors without a unique personality are judging me.
Desire   is   the
      pursuit   of   variety—
            drug   induced   vitality,
reluctantly   meandering   to   work   with   a
    slave   mentality.

No matter what they tell you young blood, life is not an endless party.
Life is a psychotic cyclical struggle, constant psychological warfare. *EP work family, etc.*
        And we're competing for what?
            To be a living large smut
villain
    civilian
chillin   in a high-interest mortgaged
mansion, cult leader like Kalki

or
CHARLIE-THE-FUCKIN-MANSON

Victim of self-centered enhancement.

I'd rather move to the northern region of the Land of
    Disenfranchisement,
meditate with smudge sticks under peyote visions writing unappreciated
    esoteric texts,
Shit...I'm living just to see what happens next.

The Crosshairs

I'm caught up in the crosshairs
of the State Department's version of justice
I trust that I'll die by thirty
so fuck this verse it gets worse
every day living like a dirty slave
at minimum wage
I try to smell the northern New Mexican sage
but all I whiff is the transplant gringo's industrial shit
the artistic chains locked around my swollen brain
has been washed from television
privately funded public education and religion
it's time to make a seminal decision
to live on my peripatetic feet
or die on my skeletal scarred knees

I'm caught up in the crosshairs
Of the State Department's version of justice
I'd search for escape
but I think it's too late the trap set by the state
can only be destroyed by monogamous hate
love doesn't exist
"...if the glove doesn't fit, you must acquit..."
what kind of shit is that
the man was on trial in Amerika cus he's black
but customarily let off cuz his pockets were fat
It's rich against poor known as Class War
working overtime without a dime
means you're fuckin poor
you can fix-up your car
hang out at your local seedy bar
but in the front lines of your own subsidized
persecution you ain't getting too far

everywhere you go there's a camera in your grill
every other commercial on television is another
advertisement for another pill that makes you iller
than before Big Brother started acting like your mother
it's like a jungle everyday but I don't
need to wonder shot down asunder
if I make one kind of blunder
they will unfairly declare
GAME OVER
Gotta stay sober
clear your mind
and you may find
a way to defeat fear
without getting it
from behind

They want you to go to jail
so They continue to set excessive bail
I'll do anything I can to kill the man
by rotting tooth or chipped nail
You say who is They
well They are those
that wear fancy clothes
and stifle everything you say
and join rifle associations
and promote right-wing white supremacy
like the N-to-the-R-to-the-A
They are the familiar familial businessmen
setting the price for outdated goods and shoddy service
They are They that make you nervous
Sadomasochistically strapped
into an inadmissible polygraph
I just laugh
cuz if you appear to relax
They can't do the math
They are them that play all day
while you work without reason

They are They that say
You've committed treason
Fuck patriotism and psychological hypnotism
They are those that feast off the beast
while you die in the bosom
I'll cut a throat if it means
I can control what I wrote
I'll massage a gun
if I don't have to run
I'll play hide and seek
for I am the meek
urban guerilla warfare son
you fighting for the concrete
ain't a damn thing fair
step up and see if I care
It's time we make plans
to rendezvous almost every night
It's time we do this fuckin thing right
If your gonna fight someone
bigger than you
you betta know
what to do
organize and devise
unorthodox ways to protect each other
from home invasion
be a sneaky little fuck like an Asian
I'm about to peal a poisonous banana
and practice the stamina
bestowed upon me by peyote spirits
not a shaman but a
raw man doing what I can
to destroy the plan
written out in the book of life
destiny is a puta
spread out on all fours
I'd call her a whore
but I suspect she's something more.

Strip Joint Politics

Strip joint politics.

Big hairy dicks, tiny pricks,
        beaver ticks,
        triple xxx flicks,
hidden camera beneath
her invaginated clit;

Nicotine
        Freelance
                Photographer...
talk   talk   talk
blah   blah   blah

left alone in shit.

Finance
        Organization
                Superiority
cow-tow hierarchy

I prefer illogical anarchy.

Illegal dust,
                board meeting bored,
Social Security Bar Code
Bouncer Maintenance
wrong priority,
direct your energy to lethargy.

High-heel onlooker
Generic prescription shareholder

Intelligent mediocre hooker.

It's over.

Catastrophic   Atrophy
This   is   nothing   more   than   an
                              R-rated
                    Pornographic Fantasy.

I'm important,
identifiable infantile insecticide
of nationwide apathy.

She's dumb.
          I've discovered more flavor
in a previously chewed withered rotting plum.

Here is your task…
          meet your quota
          and one day you too
          may be carved in the
          hills of South Dakota.

I'm trying to be
          strictly business
like an insignificant idiot taking myself serious.

Motherfuckin hypocrites…

Strip joint politics.

The Progressive

If you're dying of thirst
shoplift a 40oz bottle,
you don't need to be
a potential recruit of Earth First,
dash out the door like The Flash,
slam on the gas, hit it full throttle,
when you get home
empty the beer in a sink,
ain't no need to think
when you're already living in fear.

Lock the front and back doors,
discover a quiet room to concentrate
where you won't be interrupted;
remember…
you're engaged in an insurrectionary
task where the container is a flask
that could leave you dismembered.

Pledge of Allegiance Revised

I pledge ignorance, to the cash,
       of the Police State of Amerika.
And to the fascism,
       For which it stands,
one empire,
       under a White Christian Hateful God,
            invisible,
with incarceration and submission
              for all...

The Resistance

Not one tear escapes from my eye,
every time an Amerikan soldier dies.

Why.

...because the Amerikan soldier is a coward...
covered in shields of paranoid attire
in order to avoid the bloodshot kiss
of enemy fire...

Full-length body armor.

Not one tear escapes from my eye,
every time an Amerikan soldier dies.

Why.

...because the Iraqi fighter is a martyr...
clothed in rags, sandals, and head wraps
in order to avoid the aggressive deathtrap
of an enemy rat...

Full-length body attack.

Wars are always created then perpetuated through deception and lies...

Not one tear escapes from my eye,
every time an Amerikan soldier dies.

The Eleventh Commandment

Thou shall not conform!

...to your right-wing ways of playing it safe and silent when a violent
    sector of your degenerate culture wages war on indigenous people
    of brown skin, whether in Columbia, Palestine, Iraq, or within the
    vulnerable borders of your barbaric empire.

I fire bomb with insubordinate words like environmental militants
    visiting Monsanto subsidiaries. There is no way to stop me. Even
    when death is near...

Thou shall not conform!

I refuse to live life in fear! I resist with my scarred fist in the black clouds,
    throwing birds with middle finger as the proud crowd of republican
    disciples linger at public events, pledging allegiance to stupidity,
    singing jingoistic anthems written by socialists.
It makes no sense...

Conformity is the offspring of ignorance.

Liberal apologist, when you order me to submit my writing for
    censorship approval before lambasting condescending opinions,
    I find it deplorable how you defend the dictator's ubiquitous
    dominion.

We are being lied to and spied upon.
Every answer you thought you ever had was wrong.
Songs and prayers and rallies of protest are good,
Yet, they do nothing for those dodging bullets in the hood.
So when you tell me to behave, watch what I do and say,
I respond accordingly that I am not a slave.

I may not have had a choice the day I was born,
But I do know one thing for sure...

Thou shall not conform!

There will be no jeweled tiara in my impractical utopia.
Laws were made by rich folks to be broken by rich folks. Private property
     means nothing to me. "Ah me no have no friends, in a high society."
     The greatest threat to liberty is homeland security. This is not your
     home nor is it your land; though I have no immediate recondite plan
     I cram and study every night, formulating the best way to fight your
     systematic oppression of my contumacious expression.

Do not command me to wait in line.
Do not force me to swallow your capitalist swine.
Do not try to enlist me or convince me that your mercenary army is
     fighting for my freedom.
Do not attempt to submit me to your imperialist kingdom.
Do not praise me in the hopes of seeking my compliance.
Do not speak to me about the irrefutable truth of science.

The only proof I need that love exists are unpredictable terrorist acts of
     defiance.

How nefarious it is to think I advocate violence.
I'm just a realist. No delusional idealist notions that meditating in silence
     will aggravate the ruling elite to the point of relinquishing their
     growing power...however...
the cleverest way to overthrow them would be with a joint of the
     marijuana flower.
John Ashcroft looks helter-skelter watching Internet kiddy porn,
There is no shelter from the thunderstorm...

Thou shall not conform!

...to the federal tax extortion sucking a huge portion of my refugee
     check to patiently murder Arabs, Asians, Negroes and Latinos; there

will never be peace without justice. You want peace as long as you're on top...but the second one of us says that ain't right, you react and call on killer cop.

There really is only one solution:

WEALTH REDISTRIBUTION!

Perhaps one other suggestion:

Inspect the Unites States for Weapons of Mass Destruction

I waste in an internment camp dancing with anemic vampires
sucking sugar cane smuggled from Cuban economic sanctions
forbidding rhetorical legislation non-negotiable peace process
processing piecemeal settlements allotments of religious
manipulation pulverizing inhabitant's tenements for purposeful
extinguishments computer voter fraud hacker revolutionary
composer of contemporary blues harmonica digestion Greenspan's
inflation skyrocketing me out of my hometown. Mr. Potato Head
is a transvestite. All dues paid in praise for crazy insane mentally ill
children escaping bureaucratic maze secret social club president set
ablaze...
Molotov cocktail manuscripts published underground
only for deformed deviants organizing against the norm...

Thou shall not conform!

I can do whatever I want.
I can flaunt my impenetrable humility in the community countenance of
arrogance.
I can collect a Gila monster's hemorrhoids handcuffed to
Schwartznegger's womanizing steroids.
I can destroy my enemy with benevolence.
I can tame the rain and seduce karma to do my vindictive bidding.
I can make you think I'm serious when I'm only kidding.
I can conspire with ancestral spirits in peyote circles and abuse voodoo

to sabotage your pretty little white way of life.
I can have a dirty rendezvous with your sexually neglected wife.

Do not tell me who I am or what I'll be.
Long gone are the deceptive self-conceptions of inferiority.

My oratorical hailstorm prolixity stomps madness when I burn money
    just for fun.
Nowhere left to run. All leftists unite or perish! Cherish radical
    disobedient teachings transformed into incomprehensible action;
    how reprehensible it is to rely on reform…

Thou shall not conform!

Don't preach to me about Christ being my savior,
I won't believe it.
Don't teach me to hate Muslims and think Islam is evil,
I won't conceive it.
Don't say you're my friend willing to learn, then try to pay me to
    inform…

Thou shall not conform!

Your rules I disregard cuz I'm retarded.
Like racist Elvis Presley I shoot guns at my television airing only military
    police lawyer idiotic sitcom oriented programming.
I find beauty in what Hollywood says is ugly.
I look upon the rich with the utmost contempt.
Never, never would I show you respect just cuz you think you
    automatically deserve it.
I shoplift clothes from your downtown boutiques and give them for free
    to the meek.
I swipe food from your overstocked counters and feed the hungry
    homeless.
I snatch diapers by the dozen and donate them to single mother
    strugglers.
I operate a solitary anarcho-syndicalist ring of stolen goods smugglers.

I deflate tires of obnoxious Land Rovers, Jaguars and Hummers.
What a bummer, yes, you guessed it, I'm the one urinating in you luxury
hotel swimming pools every single summer. Listen to the desperate
heartbeat of the working-class drummer…
"We build your penitentiaries / We build your schools.
Brainwash education / to make us the fools /
Hatred your reward for our love / Telling us of your God above."

There's a tattoo under my dirty fingernails that reads: (Revolt Now—
exclamation point).
I refuse to labor for minimum wage handouts or manage your bourgeois
store,
I could never rob from the poor,

Thou shall not conform!

My heroes are the likes of Gandhi, Ricardo Flores Magon and Bernadine
Dorhn…

Thou shall not conform!

I pounce on barricades and chain-link fences at G8 summits and IMF
meetings…

Thou shall not conform!

I worship no one and nothing, spraying graffiti on your federal tablets of
stone, submitting only to my integrity…

Thou shall not conform!

No suit and tie shall ever cover my naked body, nor any work force
fatigued uniform…

Thou shall not conform!

I striptease my bright orange jumpsuit sideways and backwards when picking up trash on the roadside, I even take it off as the chain-gang boss threatens he'll tell the autocratic tribunal judge about my obstreperous behavior, slapping me with one more unaffordable fine—forget about voting out the fascist sitting in the oval office—the real life Damien Thorn will continue to reign on his sanguineous throne. It's Time we topple all tyrants, especially here at home...

Thou shall not conform!

I am dangerous. I do not follow orders, obey rules, play the game, stay the same, cut my hair, compete for gold, I never, never do what I am told. In the sick human world of psychological warfare and resource domination, I am the lonely voice of resistance and liberation. It is so simple to know what's right without moral obligation. I am the invisible that must never be found. The sound you hear, the feeling you fear. The moment for one last uprising draws near. I can't smile for the cameras when my heart heaves sighs of hopelessness, disappointment, sadness and guilt. We built machines to help us, now we jump at their command. I do not see how expertise in mathematics makes you a genius. What the world has turned into, I can't believe this. I am womyn and man, confined by a social structure I do not understand. I feel so alone...

The only life you should ever have control over, is the life you call your own.

I spit with pleasure on your virtues of conformity
with the mightiest enormity
of uncompromising scorn,

I am no living treasure...

Thou shall not conform.

Aagghhhh!

Aagghhhh!

I am not an Amerikan!

Aagghhhhh!

I've never voluntarily pledged allegiance to a lackluster flag that
represents genocide, colonialism, racism, sexism, religious lunacy,
arrogance, treachery, hypocrisy, murder, theft, and greed...
...and when I didn't pledge in protest I was sent to the principal's
office, because I was not a Jehovah's Witness, referred to the
school councilor for mediocre psychoanalysis, assessment: suspension
    for a week, recommend holding back a year...
is this because I grew up in the land of the free?

Aagghhhhhh!

Love it or leave it they say—
I'm not the conqueror but the conquered
I'm the one without a corporate sponsor...
The clay I lay my weakening body over has been guarded and taken care
of by my mother and father for millenniums, way before white western
    invasion
decided a destiny must be manifested in the name of military
    molestation.
I'm staying put like a Palestinian.
Everybody else's dues are mine to pay.
I'll only depart for eternity, throwing a finger to God on Judgment Day

Aagghhhhhhh!

None of you give a shit about the indigent womyn and children in Iraq
dying and decomposing due to Amerikan depleted uranium-using
     aggression. That's why
you're here right now celebrating an abstract concept not practiced
in reality. You're more concerned about intellectualizing over
     appropriated
revolutionary spirituality, instead of planning the best way to burn the
     Bank of Amerika. To hell with all of ya! Dance around shrouded
     embers, protect your own personal agenda,
teach to compete with each other how to be the great pretender, from
     January to December, members of your local to national chamber of
     commerce will continue to
decide who lives and who dies, who smiles and who cries, who
     disseminates
honesty, who perpetuates lies, the transformation from French to
     freedom fries…

Aagghhhhhhhh!

I am not an Amerikan!

Amerikans are the stupidest people on Earth.

Why won't you admit that you've been brainwashed and conditioned
     since birth?
The accumulation of material wealth is not the definition of someone's
     worth.
Peace is not patriotic, ask Oscar Wilde—patriotism is a virtue of the
     vulgar,
viscous, puerile, the pathetic, the psychotic—
peace is an internal understanding, a relationship
with one's own waywardness, transcended into generous deference
     when interacting
with all creatures living and dead, entities inanimate and invisible, peace
     is
shared wealth with the poorest of the poor people just to barely try and
     make the

world harmonious, comprehensible.

Aaggghhhhh!

What are you fighting for?
Are you here to try and repair a corroded, corrupted system that
protects very few and leaves the many to fend on their own...
Don't you think it's time we stop acting like we're all alone, like human
    clones?
Yes we're born alone, we die alone, no one is never around
when the ground trembles at the deaf tone crescendo of our most
    desperate groan.
But that doesn't give us an excuse nor self-indulgent justification to
defend this abusive nation against right-wing pro-war demonstrating
critics, secret police agents, and liberal apologists attempting to tame
    megalopolis.
I'm glad the capitalist Acropolis is in shambles!
My encryption they'll never unscramble, because it's the truth.
You want proof? Try practicing some humility instead of acting aloof,
ignoring depravity amongst humanity in your own given community.
You want little brown children to save, to feel sorry about,
shout at Gerald Peters, Joe Schepps, Shirley Mclaine. Infiltrate the many
    moneyed
circles within Santa Fe and make every rich motherfucker pay for
    affordable housing
amongst our trailer park residents on the Southside, where none of you
    reside,
including I; quit directing your attention and precious energy towards
    the President.
He doesn't have any substantial power, he's just doing what he is told.
But if that is where your focus must concentrate, okay,
then let's do more than just yell "Smash the State!"
Let's call for a boycott of paying federal taxes, for as long as it takes,
but aid, help, protect each other when the IRS comes to collect.
The only way these perpetual wars will end is when millions of us
anti-authoritarian dissidents decide to collectively descend on
    Washington D.C.

in a unified organized way, and stay until we've pushed, pulled, schooled,
drooled, and died, used whatever tool necessary to overthrow this and
every other illegitimate administration; demolish the Pentagon's
Military Industrial Complication, destroy the Federal Bureau of
Investigation, dismantle the Federal Reservation; let us start there if
any of you truly care. The tangled web of democracy has been laid
to rest in its historically reserved bed. But I know what you're already
thinking—he's just a dreamy-eyed blinking fool that should go back
to school and learn how the system really works—well I did, and all
I learned is that those in power look upon social activists as a bunch
of self-righteous jerks.

Aagghhhhhh!

I'm tired of living in fear!
FDR was incorrect, if you have fear itself to fear than you have
something to fear.
Fear is the source of all strength.
Fear is what motivates you to go the extra length.
Fear is the skunk's suffocating stench.
Fear made the greatness of Johnny Bench
Fear was Isadora Duncan's asymmetrical step,
Fear is why at the funeral you wept.
Fear is your steadfast faith that leapt.

Aaggghhhhhh!

When are the oppositional anti-war movement specialists gonna take their
head out their ass?
Sitting on the grass in an energy circle in front of the roundhouse is about
as effective as standing at the intersection of St. Francis and Cerrillos Rd.
holding a sign that says "Vote to Impeach", "Regime change begins at home";
but hopping back on the curb when the patrolling pig yells "Get back on

the curb!"
What are you afraid of?

Aagggghhhhhhh!

Are you afraid that if you actually made a significant sacrifice,
put your pathetic meaningless life on the line, that you might actually
bring about a kind of social change that caters to everyone's needs,
not their desires or recreational activities?
Are you afraid that you might find out that you are more powerful than
what you think you might believe in?
Are you afraid that you might find out that your life is a farce,
lived by a hesitant clown that can't climb out of its costume?
Are you afraid of turning that frown upside-down?
Are you afraid of really changing the system?
Are you afraid that if more and more people behave liberated and free
    that
the world will turn into a bunch of needle injecting unclean hippie gun
    toting weed smoking naked prancing homosexual bank robbing
    outlaw junkie artist wanna-bees with no responsibility?
Are you afraid of anarchy?
Believe me, most self-entitled anarchists are unaware of what anarchy
    really is just as much as Katie Curic is unaware of what good
    journalism is.
Anarchy does not necessarily beget violence.
What are we afraid of?
Are we afraid to live?
Are we afraid to give?
Are we afraid to be?
Are we afraid to see?
Are we afraid to love?

Aaggghhhhhh!

I got a stupid suggestion; an exercise in liberty.
Let us start by using the word 'fuck' more often in our neglected
    vocabularies

of a bastard language. It is probably the only thing we have left to express our freedom. Fuck is free. Use fuck wherever you are at whatever moment, and watch how free you feel, especially when you do it in front of a bunch of dumb snobbish tight assed aristocrats or politicians or so-called authority or some fuckin idiot. Who gives a fuck. Fuck the system, and fuck the church. Fuck the individuals sitting on a higher perch. Fuck private schools and private hospitals for the rich. Fuck referring to a womyn as a bitch, (unless she's Laura Bush.) Fuck George Dubya, Collin Powell, Condoleeza Rice and Dick Cheney; all them motherfuckers that think they're so fuckin brainy. Fuck scientists that make nuclear weapons, architects and engineers that design super maximum security prisons, you know, those assholes without any kind of humanitarian, civilized vision; fuck the shepherd and the sheep, the stronger predator that preys on the weak, the followers and the deceiving leaders, fuck the NFL with it's overpriced quarterbacks and receivers; Fuck McDonald's and Michael Jordan, Kobe Bryant, Creamland, Borden; Clear Channel, GE, NBC, AOL/Time Warner, Fuck Hollywood, CNN, C-Span, and Ted Turner; fuck video games, cellular phones, television, and a special motherfuck to that fuckin pussy Jack fuckin Nicholson; Fuck my boss who almost caught me stealing and the sell-out unions, college and high-school re-unions; fuck slaving away to keep da man paid, forget and fuck even thinking about getting laid, fuck doing drugs, all the dealers, all them road hogging eighteen wheelers, SUV's, humvees, jaguars, Mercedes benzos, beamers, fuck all the people like me who are nothing but sedated day-fuckin-dreamers. Fuck your mother, father, your sister, brother, and especially your lover. Fuck PNM, Intel, Wal-Mart, Borders, Wild Oats, Whole Foods, Albertsons and cold shoulders. Fuck Boulder Colorado, Idaho, Colorado Springs, fuck anything that has to do with Neo-Nazi uprising; Fuck the Army, Navy, Air Force, and Marines...

I am not afraid to say that I do not support voluntary socio-economically forced armed forces of adventuristic sociopathic mercenaries...

fuck all of you peace advocating activists that know nothing about authentic peace, MotherFuck the crooked-ass corrupt brutalizing fuckin Police; Fuck all Gringos, Hispanics, Chicanos, Blacks, Asians, Arabs, Indians, Queers, and Lesbians, all divisive forms of identity, fuck racist economic structures subjugating brown colored people to live in urban ghettoes of high density; Fuck globalization, all forms of slavery and money, fuck thinking that your smile of denial and corny jokes about being horny are so fuckin funny; fuck censorship and electromagnetic radioactive air waves, fuck being buried in a fuckin grave; fuck those stupid shmucks that were afraid I'd say something incendiary on the mic or advocate violence, fuck all you scared little pricks for trying to keep me in silence; fuck being so selfish and your bourgeois attitude, fuck all those motherfuckin asswipe dickheads that attended the Greg Palast lecture at the Cloud Cliff Bakery that were so fuckin rude; fuck St. John's College, the College of Santa Fe, Desert Academy, Santa Fe Prep, St. Mike's, Capital High, Santa Fe High, and all the sprouting voucher social controlling institutions that are left; continue to ditch more school, fuck playing by the rules; Fuck all politicians and realtor developing businessmen; fuck all you assholes that are so preoccupied with looking important and sounding so fuckin omnipotent; fuck the Mayor and City Council for its lack of leadership, integrity, and dependence on incompetence. Fuck the Republicans and the Democrats, all you cock-sucking suit wearing bureaucrats; the Greens and Libertarians, fuck all you fucked-up systematic utilitarians; fuck your low riders and high-end restaurants, your high-priced art, your astronauts; your cats and dogs, your play it safe poems and rants, fuck your perverted interpretations of yoga, Hindu, and Buddhist chants; fuck your new age spirituality cults and your self-proclaimed higher forms of consciousness, fuck everything about you that is so fuckin pompous; Fuck The New Mexican, The Journal Rag, The Santa Fe Reporter, and all sorts of misinformation distorters; Fuck your Christ, your cross, and holy fuckin Virgin, Mohammed, Yahweh, Moses and all fuckin religions; all your capitalistic institutions of prostitution; socialism, communism, situationism, libertarianism, authoritarianism, fascism, and all forms of control, fuck political science and paying a traffic toll. Fuck voting, elections, and finance reform, the never-ending storm that swarms inside of me, my own hypocrisy and fucked-up deconstructive existential philosophy, fuck Jacques Derrida and Mr. Jean-Paul Sartre, fuck my motherfuckin broken fuckin heart;

fuck hip-hop, spoken word, the theatre of the absurd, fuck my gluttony,
sloth, vanity, and lust, fuck the truth of the matter is that I still
haven't met anyone that I can trust...fuck everything that I love that
I must forget...fuck the poetry and plays of Bertolt Brecht! Fuck
all the tourists and all the snooty boutiques, all the conformist
disestablishmentarianism freaks, the skaters, hacky sack bums, punk
rockers, Greenpeace solicitors on the Plaza, Fuck White Trash and
motherfuckin La Raza; Fuck all you pseudo intellectuals that just
love to hear yourself talk, Fuck you Angelo for not walking the walk,
fuck all you condescending, insincere double-faced rats that overuse
the word 'absolutely', all you snitch informants bending over for the
conservatives resolutely; fuck good and evil, right and wrong, Brittany
Spears' bubblegum pop songs; Fuck worshipping Elvis and admiring
John Wayne, fuck all you whiteboy rappers like Emi-fuckin-m and
House of Pain; fuck this world and my life, fuck using a gun and a
knife; fuck all the ignorant fucks that just like to read books, fuck all
you motherfuckers giving me dirty looks; fuck revolution and fuck
the status-quo, fuck all those like me with nowhere else to go.

You see, if you use fuck so many times you come to realize that it begins
to lose its vitality and meaning. It turns out that it is just another
word that means nothing.
Teach your children well how to live throughout this gastro-intestinal
spherical hell.

Aagghhhhhh!

Unoriginal thinkers seem to by abusing Emma Goldman's quote,
"If I can't dance to it, it's not my revolution" or
"It's not my revolution if I can't dance to it"
whatever the fuck.
If all you do is dance, there will be no revolution,
How can you dance in the first place if there is no revolution?
But be careful when throwing around the word revolution;

For all of you peace loving immobilized pacifist saints that are afraid to embrace
certain forms of what you've been taught is violence, especially violence to property, because you want to remain on your feel real good about yourself higher plain of morality and ethics; never use the word. Not that you do, but just in case.
Go on a hunger strike until the war is over, see if that grabs people's short attention span,
come up with some kind of goddamn plan.
For the rest of you that do abuse the term,
understand that revolution is a call to arms;
it is a form of warfare and it involves killing,
lynching, looting, executing, and all kinds of destruction.
And at the end of it all you are most likely going
to end up with a bigger tyrant in the place of the one you deposed.
That is, if you do happen to depose the tyrant.

Aaggghhhhhh!

I don't want to talk anymore.

Aagggghhhhh!

I am not going to do what I am told.

Aagggggghhhhhhhh!

We all live in Santa Fe for one and only one reason;
we've committed treason against Babylon,
and yearn to be permanently enchanted.
We live in total denial.
But when most of you arrived, you brought
with you the crap from whatever place you came from,
the urban jungle you couldn't manage.
Now look at me, look closely at me,
I'm the epitome of the tribulations and trial,
the seeds of rage you have planted...

Aagggghhhhhhh!

I know, I know, I'm just another "ANGRY" spic
who can't control his big mouth or bombastic temper.
I'm just like my ill-behaved uncouth unreasonable despotic mother—
the former mayor,
Santa Fe's vanished hope for any kind of savior.

Aagggghhhhhhhh!

I am not an Amerikan!

Being a cultural minority I've grown up always understanding that the
    United States of Amerika is not what it seems...what it portrays
    itself to be. Amerika has always been the fascist evil empire to me.
    There is nowhere on Earth that you can truly be free. Truth, Justice,
    Freedom, Love, and Peace are forces that are there, inside and
    outside of us, forces or concepts that must be handled with care,
    entities that can be achieved through temporal passages of ecstasy;
    Truth, Justice, Freedom, Love, and Peace must constantly be fought
    for, it is the only kind of war that is worth the price; and more often
    than not we must fight for these universal THINGS by not being so
    cordial, polite, and nice...

Aaagggghhhhhh!

Understand what you're up against!
Those so-called authorities holding what you might think is power in this
    mundane realm
are determined, cold, ruthless, relentless, unmerciful, sadists, psychos,
    smart, deceitful, methodical, well organized and in communication
    (something the anti-war movement is not), and overall just plain
    fuckin sick;
they don't give a shit if you bitch and complain,
as long as you don't get out of line
and take what is yours and mine.

Aaaggghhhhhh!

Time is running out, yet we don't have to work in haste,
let's just not use our time for the petty envious ideological waste.

Aaaaggggghhhhhh!

I'm disheartened by the truth that many of you still ain't got a clue...

There's not nearly enough strength in praying,
as there is in saying "Fuck You!"

Land of Disenfranchisement

Welcome all 'yea money whores
to the land of disenfranchisement;
              where ebbing angels irenically wail,
              and the sterile metropolis repeatedly prevails.
I will be your spiflicated tour guide,
my necromantic sobriquet for today
shall be Pale Horse HIS-Panic that religiously masturbates
while complaining about my job;
metaphysical existentialism is the motivation
behind my clutching stupefaction.
There is nothing New about Mexico!
One blind occasion is all you should hoard
to discover that Santa Faithless is the fakest center
in *Das Kapital's* nowhere, somewhere there must be another kind of
    kinder
world. Downtown, town down,
no brown people to be found.
Sounds of somnambulistic rubberneckers
      day tripping to the traumatizing warble of:
      "O Say Can You See" the Native's Blood between
                       my treacherous breasts?
           Delirious toxicants abscond
           from a scientific Manhattan
           project citadel in proximity,
           just to erect another Western
           Freudian obelisk—there, right
           there in the middle of the plaza—
           a lickspittle abomination commemorating
           General Washington's
           and General Kearney's
           artificial intelligence.
Under the porchmonkey umbrella shelter,

the Palace of the Governor's fortress,
remaining token Indians squat brokenhearted,
cross-legged on wooly blankets, baking beneath
the adobe shade, hawking turquoise toys,
silver chromed junkets of jewels, trumped-up
prices to satisfy the egocentric seagull's quenchless Texan
lust, just to make her think she own a piece of Santa Fad.
Forgive the greatest unrecorded genocide in history by forgetting it!
And you never wonder why they permit you to stay,
peon in their galleries, patronizing your flat ass to re-enact anti-history
through their ultra-violent stereotypical movies, as fourteen million live
    within
eighty of your ancestor's decaying ghosts, dangling from silk neck
    tourniquets
slowly swaying directly above your sweaty raven hair that's not wavy;
delicately granted as a welcome back gift by
Don Diego DeVargas and his fribbling European promenade,
during the "peaceful" re-conquest celebrated
by the inebriated masses on an arbitrary
September day. Zozobra is a demonic, maniacally Maoist hegemonic
    idea,
Black Christ colored white, like MichelAngelo's frescoes,
Burnt on an upside-down crucifix
Beginning with a lumbering devil's silly flamenco,
Because the butchered sheep roar with frivolity in all seriousness.
Your Northern casinos are sodomizing the indigent Norteno;
I guess robbing from the poor to enrich yourselves really is a virtue
    amongst
native and naturalized U.S. citizens;

                                    I'm addicted to everything,
                                    nothing is scarce…
                                    Unaware of the farce being
                                    played to the right-wing
                                    of your rotating chin…

                    Globalization will win!

For how can you see when immaculate war covers your inestimable
terminals, teaching to hate the saintly grin of Saddam & one
Osama Bin?
Follow the lead of conformity! Iron any suit, the army's only
uniform...
and join the ranks of those that cast stones without sin. Listen,
listen...
the melancholy violin is echoing a requiem
of prejudiced chagrin for the vanished
promises of Che Guevara and Ho Chi Minh.
Now look to the bitter end, always remain secure and stand pat
like an evil Christian fundamentalist.
Gratuitous hotels will house you Amerikan ho's
on your retrograding journey throughout the City of Holy Hell.
All flavors of elusive disposable domestics below minimum age & wage
will wipe
your Anglophilic shit-stained mouth for you on discourteous command:
Guatemalans to artistically scrub your urine painted high-flowing toilets;
Salvadorans to turn down your cum soaked sheets,
Nicaraguans to scour your hoity-toity dishes,
millions of Mexicans without a decent meal to eat.
Not a trickle of Keynesian economics will cover our
immigrant children's naked caked feet.
Add Santa Fucked
to the Third World paradises that are Amerisucks Latino parasites;
Nelson Rockefeller's backyard neighbor getting it from the backdoor.
United Fruit started it all,
then Levi-Strauss heard the piracy call,
now Ford Motor Co., GAP Inc., and even Farfurnugen
are catching NAFTA's omnibus down the Camino Real,
metamorphosing into the FTAA by executive disorder.
Thank you InTel for telling us what we needn't know,
our surrounding air is unbreathable,
our ground water now smells like a burnt-out microwave
and tastes like the tip of a sharpened pencil.
Sir, what alcoholic sedative would you like to order?
The New World Order is not paying for anything!

The World Bank is not paying for anything!
The World Trade Organization is not paying for anything!
The International Monetary Fund, New Trust, G8, and Federal Reserve
    are not paying!
No one seems to be praying with sincerity!
No one wants to take responsibility.
So come on, frolic and fart and sex your way to salvation,
        The oasis of Atzlan has never been part of your dope fiend

                                            asylum

        known as this greatest nation of generous greed.
        Remember the Alamo for what it was really worth;
        Let it bleed like Davy Crocket's overweight racist spleen or
        Keith Richards' forearms without a guitar,
        fanatically hooked on that Chimayo heroin—
        fantastic as September 11th heroes & heroine's
        vengeful dreams.
                Apartheid is for real,
                you comatose greasers
                don't wanna know the deal:
Santa Facade, spy vs. spic (Special Person Intrinsically Cultivated);
the Larry Deadwoods, dildo Denkos, Grand Dragon Ashcocks, and
the young lanky boy fetishist J. Edgar Hoovers of this sickly globe
        may suck my tiny skinny fettuccine dick.
At this disappearing moment, there's supposedly a contemporary
alleged historical gubernatorial campaign
between two self-proclaimed proud stupid Hispanics.
Actually, it is a capitalistic popularity contest for the highest paying pimp;
between a carpet bagging triple-chinned obese Pharisee that beguiled
the benighted majority Hispano voting population into believing he was
    one of
them while using his patriarchal imperialistic surname, publicly serving his
constituents through self-indulgent career anointments of magnanimous
disappointments; and his worthless opponent—
John Dendhal's JohnnyComeLately little bitch!
Who do you belong to?
I belong to Las Campanas & Quail Run,
        playing eighteen holes all day, no work, what does that mean?

Stay out of my tacky gated community,
        I own acres of acreage of what you thought was your
land once, you servile indigenous dunce.
I'll have you arrested by my secret beaner police of pestilential
        swine
                your own goddamn kind!
If you ever try to cry or lie about what is mine.
                So what if I use your drinking water to waste on my
combed lawn…
by the yawning dawns dewy opening palm,
you'll be wetting your back for the thousandth breath,
drowning beneath the effluent whirlpool like a diehard fatalistic Catholic,
back to where you belong, lungs choking
on the steaming brine bubbling from the Rio Grande of Acheron.

        Land cannot be beneficial it it's private property.
        Earth is possessed only by contaminated atmosphere,
        Life by endangered species.
        I'm an endangered specie, like every brown refugee.

Fuck you Amerika! I ain't afraid of you. I spit volcanic dust on your red,
white, and blue like a suicidal fool who just wants to be cool because
growing-up ditching public school taught me that my universal relatives
were mojows…and then I saw the enlightened truth like Buddha
passing supers to Bob Marely when my hometown of Santa Fe was
barbarically gentrified consequently segregated in less than two decades
and how my thousand year-old Chicaspatas companeros were uprooted
by viral vespid weeds without roots forced by the barrel of eastern
seaboard highfalutin polluted erudition and the missile of greenbacks
stacked and stored in federal computer files requiring fingerprints
forced to the outskirts of the city's limit urban sprawl became survival
and how the cold-blooded gringo built million-dollar mansions on the
greener eastside of town where the grass constantly renews it's green
during stage three water warnings for the rest of us locos conserving our
starving children's tear drops by bathing once a week so the carefree
tourist can shower three times a day are you aware of the chamber
of commerce wielding power inflating the cost of a home the cost of

voucherless education the cost of a life the cost of a guerda wife was
too much to bare for I've never met a gavacho that genuinely cared
and was willing to share his bread with me instead he subjugated my
family in his construction factory as I sweated fifteen mean hours a
day to build his manor measured in spacious Olympic lengths while I
barely crawled to my crippled trailer tin can trapped in extreme density
yearning for self-respect but learning the strength I needed to carry-on
at the rooster's cackle was gone complacently staring at the mackerel
sky ignorantly asking the impossible question why oh why did you put
me here without knowledge, justice or grace and why did you conspire
with Satan without looking Job in the face so why does the sun keep
climbing when there's no hope left why did Tom Catron churn the
Santa Fe Ring to burn the treaty of Guadalupe Hidalgo accusing me of
theft why are so many prisons being built when there isn't a system in
place to prove the guilt and why did you bless me with consciousness
only to curse me with conscience why must everybody be acting like
Pontius why do the raped Sangre de Cristo mountain foothills look like
disseminated smallpox or karposi sarcoma on the body of an African
child why did the first book I ever read have to be one from Oscar Wilde
cuz you can tell I'm all fucked up my brain feeds on chronic anxiety
give me a few more years to complete my master's degree in insanity
bestowed by Highlands University what future was everybody talking
about when I was ten how I still remember the hours I used to spend
pretending that life was good life was fine tenderly fondling G.I. Joes
learning at too early of an age the iniquitous ways of the militaristic
pipeline and then adolescence passed and bottomless I fell from what
is divine so now I live off my hate as I contemplate snorting my eleventh
line witnessing the seventh sign yet my faith continues as steadfast as
January's snow with every new year I grow closer to embraceable death
standing backwards right in front of me confronted by my doppelganger
a Chicano hermano wanna-be gangsta pointing a 9 millimeter at La Raza
Cosmica born with a deformed Roman Jewish *Arabic* nose I suppose I
insulted his machismo pride when I said nice ride and he thought I was
referring to his chick with the battered eye bruised lip silent voice but
still I'll rejoice with him and her in the here and now cuz somehow we
gonna get it together when electric barred doors slide and the razor wire
tumbles and the bucket of crabs decides to impose a moratorium on

the cannibalistic homicide the only rumble worth pursuing is with the white locust sucking every natural resource enthusiastically watching the Earth crumble and all the joto chotas scoped-out in Brownshirt fatigues and state issued clown costumes you betta stop wasting so much time on the strip tease dealing drugs extorting feminism's wayward offspring because my love is stronger than Atlas's shoulder blades, more patient than Sisyphus's sandals, more dangerous than Pancho Villa invading the wasteland on horseback, my love is more unconditional than Corporate Executive kickbacks but now the wealthy white devil waspy gringo motherfucker has us sandniggers, spooks, spics, gooks, indians and not Columbus's Indians you dumb fuck but Mother Theresa's and what's left of the Natives he's got us, us on the precipice's cusp of a quarter crescent sinking moon we've all capitulated too damn long in the shantytowns, the landfills, the townships, the reservations, the ghettoes, the barrios, the trailer cities and every type of prison beginning with what's inside your gorgeous caramel skin but it ain't about no victory it ain't about no revolution and it certainly ain't about no stinking money that doesn't even exist. All it's about is understanding the gist behind Amerika's Neo-Nazi McCarthy blacklist, getting pissed, insist on your right to raise your fist during the singing of the national anathema, praising that coquettish harlot Old Glory, please do not enlist, do not sell-out the illegal tryst, and persist like a dadaist exorcist executing the conspicuous mist of another Aryan brotherhood member such as Rehnquist, and always, always: resist...RESIST...everything you were ever taught, temptation of being bought...resist!

I will not participate in the paper chase with the Nothing Race...
I will not participate in the paper chase with the Nothing...
I will not participate in the paper chase...
I will not participate...
I will not...
I will.

My Beautiful Palestinian Brother

My beautiful Palestinian brother,
I deny the mesmeric dream, parading images of your warped and
    wrapped
dead body, levitating just above the dirty bloody knuckles of your family,
floating down the howling canal of countenances invested eternally in
death: the only freedom.

You are beautiful my Palestinian brother,
for love is the mission of those who fight back the providential shackles
inoculating us since objectionable birth, leaving a glorious harvest for the
oppressed raindrops provocatively dripping on forbidden fruit.
Love is defined as dying for something or someone you will never know.
You fight the way I want, the way I cannot.
Unlike you I worship my bleached warlord—giver of incarcerated
disappearance of what life shouldn't be. I consciously subject myself
unwillingly to the ridicule, the unpardonable lies that are profit...and yet...

I profit nothing from Legba's seductive covenant.

You understand that you are already dead my Palestinian brother,
the apocalyptic future harbors no security for society,
endlessly occupied like a narcotic obsession, or a suffocating gerbil.
    Threats of permanent displacement, police pissing on our program of
expression without commercialism, commerce dominates the pubic policy
that transformed like a Decepticon into intolerable bureaucracy,
    preventing the blind from seeing in an asphyxiated sphere; my heart
holds more holes than the late great Earth's ozone, while polar caps
    melt as
fast as Hal Lindsey followers learn how to ruin home with trickle down
tyrannies and Harvard Business School paradigms.
    I understand your resolved methodology. But I cannot join you.

You see I am the filthy, unorganized spic. The hermit's coward. The
    coward hiding behind Howard Stern's stern smirk of misogynistic
    benevolence; demoniacally listening
to Rush Limbaugh in an ambulatory limbo.
Though I must admit, my lovely Palestinian people, you inspire me to
    submit
no more to the perennial whore that is the forlorn Gringo, the single
Evil Empire draped in Betsy Ross's crusty panties.
How do you maintain through the infiltrating pain of tainted blood
    beneath
your bare feet? Tossing spontaneous stones at Amerikan made tanks, as
    they
reenact the blitzkrieg. Shooting with booby-trapped bought pistols
from Israeli soldiers, while they, covered in holistic bulletproof attire fire
pinpoint missiles from Apache helicopters, supplied by the U.S.A—the
Unilateral Satanic Association.

Never forget to always burn a flag for me, I won't regret it!

With your blistering cuticles, caked palms, and besmirched fingernails
    you
represent the burdened dissident that is the brown being. Sucking on a
Winston, oblivious to your advertent, bloodshot oculus. Praying during
    the
hummingbird night for tranquility, as the playful enemy unveils its night
    vision—
technology's wonderful underworld of darkness.
We may be at an indecorous disadvantage, but at least our posterity will
remember that *we* were not the savage.
I love you my beautiful Palestinian brother...
        Hierosolyma has never known such a bewitching martyr,
        the wretched of the planet plotting imploding lamentations
        and the divided United Nations still has no authority.
I love you because you understand more than any of us the
    worthlessness of
this white world:

Volcanic arsenals of mass destruction present us with the ignis
fatuus of peace; Cannibalistic requirements ordain the twilight
idea success has taught us to misunderstand; Scientists caped
in white thick frocks concentrate on creating cancerous products
called food; Bioengineering is the crystal particles swarming
circular in my tortilla; Human cloning and mindful conditioning is
the fateful reality devised to wipe out the incalculable homeless;
Sweatshops scatter all over the thirdless world while the Fourth
Reich marches forward in the New York Cock Exchange, NASDAQ
= Niggers and Spic Darkies Are Questionable, and the Slick
& Perverted 500 scurrilously joining the 700 Club to become
dismembered members of the Fortune 500…

I profit nothing from Legba's sacred covenant!

You cry out to me my Palestinian sister and brother,
        but I am deaf like a contemptuous Ludwig.
You cry out to me
        but I turn the other cheek for I'm a sadomasochistic Christian.
You and I have more in common than a doddering wasp and a
disoriented bee,
        but love only works from a distance.
Your persistence enables me to see clearly the lie that I've been living.
The consecrated ground you retreat over has been stolen from your
unassuming eyes,
The obscene city of Unholy Faith has been stolen from my forgiving
        tears,
The Nubian Jesus bled for nothing.
Your purified water and communal land has been taken from your
        collective
disagreement; dry deserted desert water here is furtively regulated to
        shelter
finicky conglomerate hotels, along with Jack Nicklaus' designed
golf courses with the whip scars scaling the chaffing color de café back of
castrated angels, making a temporal pyramid for permanent residents of
        hell.

The Nubian Jesus bled for nothing.
In 1948, your fate was hijacked by a murderous state,
self-righteously claiming ownership to terrain stained
with hateful blessings bestowed by a crooked biblical book.
In 1846, our indigenous light eclipsed, we all got licked
by deceitful Amerikan settlers legally encouraged to shoot, rape, and
    lynch.
Up to date in Santa Fake, the enchanted city that is supposedly different,
tourism is terrorism in its imperfect imperialistic form.
The perverted Gringo was drawn to our once brown town in search of
    New Age
spirituality, only to parasitically squash the human soul.
Gentrification, racist gerrymandering, and exponential high-end
    development have
each taken their reactionary toll.
The white locust swarmed in and out and all around downtown, painted
    it
brown, moved the brown people out, to the subjacent Southside where
    the
sewer treatment plant patiently resides. Every day I live in open shame,
in disseminating, circumcised rabbit hutches. Every day I need a crutch.
It feverishly distresses me to confess this much to you my strong
    Palestinian brother.
Please forgive my abstinence, absolve my disobedience to Allah.

Never forget to always burn a red, white, and blue flag for me, I won't
    regret it!

This Mohammedan minority is no priority of apriority authority!
We are living in fear, dying in captivity!
The church of the Nativity will never save a native!
The only gray hope is the creative thought of those who can't be bought;
seeking elaborate urban tunnels to escape getting caught,
wrought with anxious frustration, looking for elusive liberation but
only finding it when one of us is shot.
Time cannot stop a common cause resistance to the occidental ethnic
    cleansing clock.

Malcolm, Brother Minister! Encourage me every moment to attack the
   sinister
behavior of the Freemason savior. Billions of Brown People forever
   Bleed,
as the homicidal Bush syndicate extols another New World order
   genocidal creed:

"Follow the path of Neo-liberal greed, my bastard children. At Lucifer
speed you shall remain universally free in a harem of unadulterated
taboo. Mongrels of every colored race have now been erased
from the ground of Canaan. Voodoo could not save them even if
D'Angelo believed in Martin Sheen handcuffed to an illegal alien.
Mehican, Injun, Arab and African...they're all the same to me...
Whooeee...Step up and join the Army, my sacerdotal sentinel of
wanton lust, capital, and liberty. Support your country, the righteous
pimp in the face of conscientious democracy. I will create for you a
DeMoNmOcKeRy. Aks Collin Mockery. Wayne Brady may be the star
only to go so far as a slogging Porsche car driven by Drew Carrey.
I'm the demagogue, parading charity like a philanthropic whore,
trading her in for butchery when egalitarianism knocks on heavens
militarized door. I'm that same backward redneck cat that came
up with that fancy catchy new verbal attack—"humanitarian war."
I'm beyond evil and good. I'm Zarathustra low riding through yo'
hood, only to strip the barrio naked of it's wetback culture, celebrate
the vulture! Backdrop of bars and stripes designed by one more
corrupted cop. You are my backstop, I your leader. I'm the forgotten
conductor of this insane train of pro-war hate mongering cabinet of
corporate cheaters. No, Absolutely Not, I'm no deceiver. Death to all
dissenting disbelievers! I'm John Elway shuffling the pig's skin when
there's four open receivers!"

I profit nothing from Legba's sanctified covenant.
The nigger Jesus bled for nothing.

I miss you my stunning Palestinian sister...
      I miss you because I never knew you
         except in beatific landscapes, touching fingertips, waiting for the

sizzling flesh to cross the Mosque's catastrophic threshold,
scared to witness the depth of your soulless breath,
>   my mother was raped remorseless.
I love you my Sophoclean tragedy,
majesty of matriarchy returning to teach us how to disembowel
kindness
aggravating boundless miracles spreading over Magdalene's
bruised
derriere, suicide bombing is more fun than panicked dominoes
played
behind steel cages where my rage is locked and loaded and
leaden...
>   my mother was raped remorseless.
>   ...and...
John Lennon was not an exception,
he slapped Ono for her dominatrix tresses, her gold digging vibes,
her black eyes that are the hypnosis of comatose daydream
believers.
The green monkey was a Confederate
sponsored eugenic experiment, a coveted detriment to the once
lavish continent restlessly wasting in Western museum
basements.
>   AFRICA!
your weightless children will not be spared...

NOTHING CAN COMPARE TO THE EVANGELISTIC BIOLOGICAL WARFARE!

My beautiful, beloved Palestinian lover, there is no other divine
adversary of
Old Gooseberry.

No longer will we not grow stronger;
No danger will keep us from remaining intimate strangers.
Stranger and stranger sound the wishful justifications of evolution.
Machiavellian Darwinism is not the solution to the inescapable problem
of capitalistic prostitution. Long live the intifada, the Moreno revolution!
A C- student Tartuffe dictates from his diarrheic oval orifice,

while the rest captivated in wait lie to the denial of themselves,
trotting along effortlessly in their ever expanding, recreational SUV's.
Amerika calling for Israel to expeditiously pull back it's poltroonish
    offensive
is about as offensive as spic, black, and gook minorities laboring for
    Amerika's
killing machine. Milton's fallen Fiend is the drug dealer kingpin, papa
    George
Herbert Walker Bush, kissing the opportunistic reflection in his M-16's
    barrel gleam.
The one providing arms and funds is only a charmer of sadistic snakes.

All praise due to Hamas—feeding your children, medicating your sick,
    while the PLO
sucks the Likud's wrinkled soggy dick,
        negotiating peace contracts to fence you in electrically,
        we don't need anymore parliamentary pricks playing politics.
Handouts for the poor will never settle the injurious, incurable score.
Keep fighting back with stubborn hospitality,
        civilian setbacks,
    unexpected uzi raids on those
        that think they got it made.
All praise due to the Al Aqsa Brigade!
All praise due to the Palestinian Islamic Jihad,
    Palestinian Liberation Front,
        and Popular Front for the Liberation of Palestine;
Please tell me you are capable
    of forming a unified team
        in order to finally overcome and achieve
            that which isn't what it seems;
                to see what is unseen.
I mean,
    the only thing the southwestern Chicano
    can do is form an insignificant temporary gang
    to spit on another clan of brothers, talk some pachuco
    slang language, cruise a cherry red low rider painted
    with narcotic dispensing or slave wage paychecks,

pick up little chicks and bitch and complain about
how Whitey came to steal their land, but none are
willing to sacrifice a hand to stand up as one voice,
                    one song,
to right the presently historic future wrongs done to us
by ourselves, and the perpetually flowing open wound puss.
Fuck what you never heard—
brown people are the absurd—
majority of the silent word—
playing unity & community for the Herb—
keeping each other down like Muslims and Kurds.
All praise due to Hezbollah Party of God—
        ain't it odd how the U.S. second-guesses
the underdog strength of the strong
        always getting it wrong
underestimating the struggle of
        guerilla units like the Viet Cong.
Only we will be the ones to say where we belong!

All praise due to the Basque Fatherland and Liberty—
        may the fascist Euro-trash country of Spain
        forever feel the pain they inflicted on your sacred name.
All praise due to FARC—Revolutionary Armed Forces of Colombia—
        how dare the dismissive hypocrisy of Washington D.C.
        declare you as narco-traffickers when Pfizer, Bristol Myers Squib,
        Johnson & Johnson, the Amerikan Medical Association, and the
            Bush
        skull & bones cartel been dealing paralytic devastating drugs to
        Amerikan civilians for centuries.
All praise due to Revolutionary Organization 17th of November, the
    Revolutionary Peoples's Liberation Party/Front, the Revolutionary
    People's Struggle, Sendero Luminoso, the Zapatista EZLN, Tupac
    Amaru Revolutionary Movement, Mumia Abu-Jamal and
John Walker Lindh;
At least this racist Mexican won't forget Lori Berenson,
locked up in a concrete cell full of Vladimiro Montesinos veterans,
those superfluous Fort Benning trained good Samaritan CIA operatives.

All praise due to the Israeli Refuseniks, praise due to the hunted manic
depressive Abbie, and the only enlightened homosexual seraphim Allen.
A very special shot out to Rachel Corrie of International Solidarity—
for choosing not to ignore the injustice and suffering any more.
you gave your young White Western privileged life to put an end
to Israel's policy of demolishing makeshift construction with
intentional bulldozer malfunction.

If there were more of you, then the nimby Gringo would have already
achieved
delicate integration, without impalpable borders guarding *their* terroristic
Nations.

A terrorist and terrorism means resistance by people who aren't going
to be cowed, according to the United State's sweating brow, and the
Universal Chomsky Intellectual Dictionary for Uncompromised
Visionaries.

My Delphian Palestinian brother,
from Iberia to Atzlan, Palestine to Tenochtitlan,
we have always shared the same, unbreakable bond holding the one
and only magic wand.
My breathtaking Palestinian sister,
with your nauseating, inartificial beauty you blow yourself up to prove
that feminism is not flaunting your pumped boobs on the televisitation
tube, and in the chauvinistic process getting paid demented millions like
Jennifer Hopeless in a Clintonesque pink power fuckin suit,
still receiving more or less of the devil's patriarchal pie.

No more will I ponder the unanswerable question, why.

My beautiful Palestinian brother,
you are Monsignor Oscar Romero,
riddled with ridiculous myriad bullets made in the U.S. of A,
released from controllable, vicious cannons held by bashful assassins,
trained to reign in the great plains of sacrificial spilt blood,
echoing Allende's communist innocence…

trained to dominate this scarred Earthly domain with intolerable, insufferable,
excruciating, agonizing, harrowing, racking, tearing, tormenting, torturing,
Pinochet tactics of inflicting everlasting pain
in the carnivorous name of National Security.
All praises due to those bloodthirsty, trigger happy soldiers and
patrolling pigs trained in the greatest nation of the U.S. of A!

Don't forget to piously burn a red, blue, and white flag, colored with scars and
hype, especially dedicated to me, my mentoring Palestinian brother, mother,
father, and sister, my brown family.

Behind your kaffiyeh shroud, I know you
are as handsomely undaunted as Zapata, Pancho Villa, Chico Mendez, Che
Guevara, Joaquin Murieta, Dolores Huerta, Ricardo Flores Magon, Valentina Ramirez,
Comandante Ramona, Subcomandante Marcos, and touchingly, touchingly...
Thomas Miguel Benidicto and Debbie Jaramillo—
family for celestial infinity—
ironically juxtaposed and trapped in the Puritan, Protestant, Pederastic tiny
pediculous megalopolis of pedophilic filthy faith.

I profit nothing from Satan's staphylococcal covenant!

In the beginning there was the word...that is my only weapon;
my only crucified, untouchable belief that is the sanctimonious lie...
No more will I ponder the unanswerable question why,
No more...no more...what for and why?

Part II

Hitler is a Jew! Who? Adolf: furious Fuhrer of furor. The delinquent
messiah flippantly yelling at overpopulated concentration camps
in the Gaza, West Bank, Bethlehem, the Ramallah, circulating open
palm pamphlets and Chaplin's Lilliputian mustachio, swapping his
ashen swastika for a perverted Pentecostal hexagram. Thus spoke that
cantankerous, fat-ass hardcore Zionist porn star Ariel Sharon…
Velcome, Velcome, velcome, velcome, to the concrete jungle centralized
within pandemonium. Platinum Rolexes is not enough to consecrate
the frivolous difference between the pagan sexes. Ask not and you
shall receive the cabalistic evil that has the access to nuke your infidel
Kaaba, with the backward desire of a Duke of Hazard. Wave the Dixie
when the Devil goes down to Georgia, or I'll still make you squat in the
back of the bus. Fuck Rosa Parks! She was a certain nobody we built
a home for in a trailer trashcan. The Nazi is your habitat for humanity.
The Nazi is a Jew. The Nazi is Henry Ford, J.D. Rockefeller, Andrew
Carnegie, William Hearst, DuPont, just to name the few best of the
worst, ohh…I thought you knew. The Nazi is your blessed mother. The
Nazi is the Holy Trinity. The Nazi is the restless many succumbing to
the prosperous few. The Nazi is the devil worshipping motley crew that
will rule this goddamn planet for as long as I can't stand it. The Nazi
is your deadbeat father. Don't bother rebelling, resisting, I'm the only
Amerikan to keep persisting on a globalization of economic devastation.
The Nazi is the stupid-ass flag waving Amerikan, not caring about
those ho's who suppose the frozen ice cream will melt vanishing in
their Latin shanty towns telling intangible tales secured in a spiritual
commune of corrections. There is not enough time to correct all of our
bistered mistakes that turned out to be flaccid erections…who would
have ever thought the Jew should take my place? I hail you, my basidial
Jewish descendant. You storm the stacked, cramped tenement boxes
of sandniggers begging you to burn their scarce belongings. Old bitchy
womyn wail their scarves off as you scarf the remainder of their Uncle
Ben's uncooked corporate rice. The way you scream and scoff at their

desperate pleas, reminds me of the time I took off all your clothes and coveted your wrinkled, putrid flesh, and made you jog forever in the circle of nothingness. Oh, what blissful memories. My chosen Jewish offspring, you possess more malevolent generosity than Bill Gates. Abandon all hope, yea who enter nirvana's fortified gate. I knew some day you'd learn how to hate. Isn't it great? No fate can be richer, than the manifest destiny of the stormtrooper…the one and everlasting virtue of the celebrated executioner. Wear that Star of David with Apollyon's saintly angelic pride. Religiously devour the swine of the brownskin. I'll be crucified like an unidentified thief if you don't win! Why, you're better than I ever was. You murder international Red Cross workers that claim to be neutral…there's no neutrality in war. You even barricade the road to the wounded. Let them bleed, let them blow, may the intoxicated wind pretend no longer to be our solitary friend or foe. I am so fond and proud of your progressive politics. Practice more at shedding innocent blood that the upside-down Koran licks, the Rastafarian Bible tricks. I nearly disbelieved it myself—a grandiose toast, to the betterment of health for the ethnocentric—you even utilize a gentle German shepherd to evacuate thousand-year-old Gentile settlements. The Jew has become a Nazi, finally. Now you are the pioneering cowboy, rounding up sable people branding numbers on their contaminated forearms. I never knew you were so Anti-Semitic. Welcome to the Aryan race of rats wasting! You finally traded in your gold-plated menorah for a blazing pitchfork. If I only could have grasped the intrinsic value of your sold soul. I knew you were always scum, but never would I have surmised that one dawn you would voluntarily bang the tin drum. If I only could have seen the serene contours of your pale pigment, it wouldn't have been just a misguided figment of my twisted imagination to construct such a promising young terminator. I could have recruited all of you, instead of reluctantly marching you towards your maternal incinerator. If I only knew, if I only knew. If I only chose to truly understand the Jew…if I only knew…"

How could you? How could you Israel, forget the Final Solution, the 1940s European Holocaust, where no one came to your aid, not even the shameful U.S.A, how could you forget the 4-6 million martyrs that died in the name of your rotten, barbaric, misbegotten future. How the fuck could you?

I love you.
I love you my beautiful, bold, beloved Palestinian brother.
I witness the fragile caress of your brethren kiss your traumatized skull,
whispering in a roar as your frigid body cascades above the intrepid
    mob.
Wave the black, the green, the red...carry your tattered clothes,
your torn flag into the final battle of Armageddon,

There is always a grave waiting...

The Day George Herbert Walker Bush Died

The day George Herbert Walker Bush died...
I experienced peace on Earth for the first and only last time.

The majority moreno people of the first third world prison
were finally liberated,
epileptically dancing
through de-militarized timeless zones;
all alone in Galeano's upside-down universe,
still not defeated by the Millennium Brown Shirt extinguishments here
    at home.

That half-second when George Bush passed
was a getting high Mick Jagger singing
Jumping Jack Flash kind of gas.
The greatest **EVIL** humyn kind has ever never wanted to know
left an unremembered embroidered memory of unremitting
decomposed mist, leaving it to
retarded posterity to rabidly undermine
the authentic international community,
wolfishly hoping to accomplish that not so quite nor
quiet no more white devil worshipping Christian goal of world
    domination.

When daddy Bush croaked,
I cracked an unapologetic omnipresent joke
on how peace now meant something much more
than petite bourgeoisie offspring
        pounding hog-skinned stolen drums out of rhythm,
        unconscionably careless about ripped-off culture,
        those damn face-painting, neo-hippie uncouth vultures,
          frivolously
        rebelling against my sugar-coated embarrassing inheritance,

slothfully surviving off of this much needed appreciated
trust fund...seaweed eating hypocrites.

We're coming to Amerika!...where the whited sepulcher mercilessly
  reigns with
impunity, without responsibility, but with Arthur Anderson accountability
and Pecksniffian moralistic virtue. Don't you too want to be one of us?

But now that papa Bush is pushing bio-engineered daisies...
  Peace means: tiny children in India won't have to be chained to
               multi-tasty smoking beedies, bartered into slavery at
               the age of five watching how their mothers prostitute
               themselves to stay alive as the nuclear beehive in
               Kashmir was contrived to support a puppet institution
               of impressive repression so you the best in the West
               can worry about what soiree you will attend tonight,
               while billions in India don't have to worry about leaks
               for they have no shelter except in their own feces.
               Thank our Lutheran God India is an ally. We need to
               give them more military money and steal their brainy
               talented computer jocks and engineers to contribute
               to our overly developed oligarchic economy.
  Peace means: Africa becomes our number one top unquestionable
               priority. When Bush died everybody finally decide to
               arise from their high-financed self-inflicted
               government controlled slumber and realize hundreds
               of millions of numbers infected with AIDS in the
               motherland is due to the deliberate, pre-determined,
               premeditated, intentional genocidal murderous
               injection of the HIV virus into little starving babies,
               starving breast sagging mothers, skeletal starving
               adolescents, skinny starving young middle-aged old
               womyn and men, entire familial generations...all
               through the charismatic, colonialist charitable
               costume of smallpox vaccinations administered by
               vicious Great Britain, designed by yours untruly: the
               U.S.A—The Unilateral Satanic Association. Yes you

ignorant, feigned subjugated citizenry of heartfelt disgust…you trust your ruling class and so-called government so much that you choose to turn the other cheek when it comes to understanding and indubitably knowing that HIV/AIDS was the gracious fascist's cold wet dream; chemistry's formulated welcomed nightmare to produce Pandora's capitalistic, optimistic, opportunistic most distinguished biological weapon ever. Under the loving beguiling guidance disguise and psychopathic pathetic leadership of one George Herbert Walker Bush as head of the CIA , Amerika the Ugly gave diplomatic birth to AIDS in a laboratory. Depopulation programs do exist. Depopulation programs are for real. Depopulation programs are the menacing brainchild of Henry Kissinger, George H.W. Bush, Colin Powell, Donald Rumsfeld, Ronald Regan, Dickhead Cheney, and take your prick out of Amerika's historic most celebrated and honored right-wing religious fundamentalist republican elitist redneck sons-of-bitches Neo-Nazi Klu Klux Klan Aryan Brotherhood upper upper-class middle-class ultra-conservative, plain old conservative, somewhat conservative centrists liberals and Democrats. Thank you all for contributing to the perpetual myth of the green monkey fornication.

For every person that dies of AIDS in Africa, I issue an incontrovertible voodoo hex, a Yaqui curse on the affluent Anglo-Saxon children of Europe and Amerika: may your days here in hell be blessed and pleasant ones; may you have every material thing you want, and may your hours be filled with dancing, singing, chanting, praying, fucking and carefree innocence. Your lives are well worthless, without meaning. That is why you are the way you are. Quit searching for yourself and search for someone else. Your soul was sold a long time ago…

The day daddy Bush died,

Amerika was no longer.
The stronger savage barbarian mentality disappeared,
    universal fear desisted as the sole motivation for selfish survival.
The U.S.A died as well,
    hell became heaven,
    fifty outdated states divided,
    united decidedly for everyone's integrity,
    unleavened leavened bread
    was shared amongst the
    living dead for one forgetful moment,
    no salivating opponents, just harmonious components
    of eternal solidarity, maternal lessons
    to stress the unflawed importance in
    sacrificial generosity.

                        The day daddy Bush died...
        oil, **OIL!**–that bullyragging
        excuse to systematically reduce the
        humyn population of Arabs, was never
        again used by clever innumerous fools
                in the polluted hemisphere's West,
                claustrophobically suffocating
                through suicidal mechanical
                death tools.
        oil, **OIL!–PETROLEUM!**
        We don't need it. Who here will toil
        endlessly to seed psychotic road rage by
        bleeding more Palestinians, Iraqis, and
        Iranians than squeamish vampire bats
        biting one-legged crickets incapable of
        making prohibited love?
        Fuck Wal-Mart and its non-unionized monopolized
        gulag of retailing harmful unnecessary plastic crap!
When the schmuck Bush patriarch gasped his final breath...
    nothing was left of the Killing Machine you unctuously identify as
    Israel.
    What else were they required for but to be Babylon's golden calf

worshipping monetary whore.
The distorted heroic memory of Ben-Gurion was scorned, burned
from your brains like the Amerikan flag during festive holidays on a
    public
square in Tehran, where it doesn't ever have to rain. Perhaps not as
    beautiful
as Homa Darabi on February 21, 1994, defiantly tearing off her headscarf
    and
long coat, blanketing herself in highly flammable petrol,
igniting her untarnished spirit on fire and admonishing to life patriarchal:
    "Down with tyranny, long live freedom!"
Ahh...what fierce beauty; what impecunious yearning...
    but yet also and still, the Amerikan flag is almost as beautiful
    when it is grilled...the Amerikan flag is always beautiful when
    it is burning.

The day George Herbert Walker Bush died
was the day the war on Afghanistan ended.
Caspian Sea Oil and Natural Gas reserves
is the only reason the likes of Bush and Cheney
committed respectable treason in Halliburton fashion.
Don't you sleepless sheep feel more than 30,000 Afghani civilians and
    children
murdered, maimed, destroyed, amputated, scorched, plagued,
    shot, starved, mutilated, vaporized losing a useless eye here an
    insignificant leg or two there,
hundreds of thousands of humyn beings permanently displaced from
    their homes, places of residence, is justifiable compensation for the
    president's compassionate lust to rule the world as the almightiest
    Supreme Race dunce?
Don't you understand that September 11th
was part of the same dictatorial plan to consolidate dildo Dubya's
    power?
That more than 2,800 Amerikan civilian slaves were sent to Sheol's gates
so another spoiled dumbfuck can become Chancellor of Chaos in 2008.
By the hour's sub-particles we are losing what liberties of civility
we never had...by the minute's fledglings we are all being had...

by an infinite forfeiting of freedom patriotic fad.
Insecure national security is not more important than individual liberty.
WAKE UP! MY FRIGHTENED TERRIFIED EXPERIMENTAL RATS!
Have no fear of the PATRIOT Act!
Disobey every law in the book that was not written for you,
unless of course you are one of the 1% coarse huMAN clones
closing down corporate shop,
pocketing the retirement savings of disbelieving, unthinking
laboring lambs.
What a risible goddamn sham that you actually began to consider
    Amerika as the land of the free.
How can the place that tops the list in imprisonment of its own citizens
    be referred to as the land of the free?
Nothing is free in a capitalist society!

The day George Herbert Walker Bush kicked the missile defense system
    bucket,
Everyone just said "Fuck it, I ain't got nothing to lose..."
    "Freedom is just another word for—-nothing left to lose..."
Dear Janis:
    That day poppy Bush conked, the horns couldn't stop honking,
there were no more heavy addictive heart-stopping drugs to be sold,
whether from a clinical pharmacy or a yellow-lined curbside. This was
so because the most successful businessman drug smuggling swindling
kingpin warlord was gone. There was no more of Scotty's beaming crack
to be had in black Amerikan big city ghettoes. The not so clandestine
war on Columbia to take over the coca plantations ceased and FARC
in reciprocal partnership with the Zapatista EZLN took the first step to
declare peace to free the rest of the Chicano Latins—from Mexico on
down to Magellan's insurmountable whereabouts around the southern
most tip of Chile to the Caribbean—La Raza Cosmica led the way for the
rest of the restless world, showing all that it's okay to be a homo sapien
hybrid. We really are all sisters, mothers, brothers, fathers if we want
to be with no need for religious theocracy and democracy was finally
achieved. Mumia Abu-Jamal, Leonard Peltier, Sundiata Acoli, Dr. Alan
Berkman, Tim Blunk and countless other gentle victims incarcerated due
to Amerika's vengeful, racist, capricious Criminal Court Law Enforcing

Judicial System—where the genuine righteous criminal calls the shots, and the rest of us just take it up the dry G-Spot—all of these political prisoners were set free...we began to breath again because Brazilian rainforests were restored faster than any of us could guess when science was directed to healing humynkind and her house...the seventh planet from the abyss. Nothing could stop the onslaught of nuclear disarmament, nothing could hinder the taking over of the Pentagon and shutting it down. Nothing could block the cocky insubordination of peace-loving militant disobedient savages ravagingly sabotaging CIA headquarters in Virginia's sodomized vagina. No one would stand in the way of taking over FBI Headquarters and shutting it down right after we tore down J. Edgar Hoover's nameplate and donated it to the Preservation of Historic Sadomasochists. You should have seen it; lesbians and queer men were revered because many of them decided it was time to relinquish their monocratic agenda of creating their own kind since alleged heterosexuals bequeathed their choice to listen to children as they made most of the major decisions affecting our fraudulent lives concentrating on health care, humanitarian aid, foreign policy only in the form of economic aid with no interest or debt, education, labor, law, politics, affordable free adequate housing, water & environmental protection, and many more issues of justice regarding the ascendancy of the humyn race. When George H.W. Bush died there were no longer Haitians, Taiwanese, Chinese, Indians, Indonesians, Pakistanis, Vietnamese, Koreans, Egyptians, Nigerians, Brazilians, Nicaraguans, Salvadorans, Tahitians, Philippinos, there were no longer any Asians, Africans, Arabs, Latino Americanos, or any indigenous natives of any kind corroding in sweatshops because there was no such thing as a First or Third World contaminated bus stop. Globalization vanished without a DNA trace like Fred Hampton, d.a. levy, and Lumumba. The School of the Americas in Fort Benning, Georgia was never again to be erected; the location where perfected torture taught kidnapped street children of Latin America how to attach electric plugs to testicles of liberation theologists, the place where Israeli soldiers and secret police came to receive an invaluable education on how to eradicate an entire generation of an already poverty-stricken nation...What kind of power is super when you pick on unsuspecting people that barely possess the ability to brush their tarter ridden teeth? There will be no relief for

refugees of any plutonium age, until Amerika is erased from history's
bloody page after page after page after bloody fuckin page...

The day George Herbert Walker Bush expired...
infernal fire from peace officer police violence
became quenched; even the epizootic wench
misleadingly proud to harbor a wooden badge,
joined the aphrodisiacal apocalyptic luau roasting the
profane heralded guest he once was.
There was no more machine-like fuzz
to perpetuate the injudicious hate
of the richest of the rich.
The police now protected us,
those the same as themselves,
those they swore to uphold,
those about a divorced troubled life they have no hold over;
so they only seem to consistently complain with invincible melancholy
    pain.
The day George H.W. Bush kicked off...
inhumane sanctions forbidding Iraq and Cuba
to feed, clothe, and inoculate its population
        were lifted. 5,000–6,000 Iraqi children a month
        died due to the sorry loser ex-president's
        gift of tormenting psychological and physiological destruction.

There were never ever any more pre-emptive illegal international acts of
    aggression.

That same day
too many U.S. troops were removed from Saudi Arabia
and in the holy land you didn't get a hand chopped
for trying to steal a forbidden apple;
        there was never again a bullet popped,
            a not so smart bomb dropped,
                nor Molotov cocktail released
                in the Middle East;

The day George Herbert Walker Bush died...
peace became the only way of the anthropomorphic beast.

The moment George Bush departed,
every brokenhearted citizen
of the oppressed dimension farted.
The Bhagavad Gita constantly on the con-of-science
of J. Robert Oppenheimer—*"Now we become death, shatterer of worlds"*
was given no more or less value than
the indispensable tutelage of the affectionate feudal lord fugitive Dali
    Lama,
anything other than the asinine King James version
recreating the bible unholy.
Didn't you know that the Black Panther Jesus was a hard-core
    communist?
The day daddy Bush bit the eroding dust...
everybody remembered the Bush first fucked-up family
historic saga of squalid criminality:
        —we remember how granddaddy Prescott Bush knowingly and
            willingly served as a money launderer for the Nazis.
        —we remember that Brown Brothers was the Bush heritage
            Amerikan money channel into Nazi Germany, and that Union
            Bank was the secret pipeline to bring Nazi money back to
            Amerika from Holland.
        —we remember how granddaddy Prescott Bush was a director of
            a New York bank where rich Germans and Amerikans who
            supported the Nazis, Amerikans such as Charles Lindbergh,
            stashed millions in personal wealth.
        —we recall that George Dubya Bush's domestic agenda as
            "compassionate conservatism", was formulated by the
            CIA's Manhattan Institute, and that the Manhattan Institute
            is a right wing think tank founded by former CIA director
            William Casey who helped bring thousands of former Nazis
            to the US following WW II, placed them into directorial
            positions within the agency to recruit and train agents, and
            these same Nazis are the ones that helped establish the
            School of the Americas, and the entire post-modern policing

superstructure/network across Amerika from the Atlantic to the Pacific. In other words, every kind of cop is nothing but a corrupt gangster, a wholehearted, brainwashed dedicated Nazi. Take a look at their uniforms, especially their fancy dandy caps.

—we recall that George Herbert Walker Bush in the early 1970s, vehemently worked with David Rockefeller in promoting a worldwide depopulation program.

—we recognize the current Bush administration's direct ties to vaccine and drug manufacturers; and why so many of Dubya's cabinet members are former drug company executives: what do you think is the connection between these ties and the Bush family's seventy year long documented involvement with eugenics and population control?

—we acknowledge that daddy Bush and brothers Jeb, Neil, and George have 25 super secret bank accounts worldwide, through which they have laundered tens of billions of dollars of illicit funds that they siphoned from television hypnotized Amerikans, from drug trafficking, from weapons smuggling and illegal gold and diamond smuggling overseas…Nigga please…

—we already know that George Herbert Walker Bush and the sweet devilish children were personally acquainted with would be presidential assassin John W. Hinckley.

Remember this unabashed non-conspiratorial truth, and seriously contemplate
who the real terrorist is and terrorist networks are.
For this is not even the beginning.
It is impossible to forgive when you forget,
for how can you know what you are supposed
to be forgiving.

The day George Herbert Walker Bush died…
there were no more spies,
but more than enough of a surplus of

necessary supplies to feed, clothe, and house
the every growing already too many homeless and hungry.
No more lacerating tear drops were discovered in the
itching eyes of Sierra Leone womyn and children;
the geographical region where more African people suffer forever,
permanently crippled, dismembered, and
butchered. Hopping to the mine on half a leg
or none, hugging, lacking a muddy elbow
or an entire arm or two, more than capable
of feeling, meaning and expressing to their
enduring family that never abused sentiment
amongst the world's poor: "I love you."
All this in the millions, so you hideous Gringos
in North Amerika and Europe may indecorously
ornament yourself with flashy diamonds around
your bony fingers, shimmering diamonds hanging from
your stringy necks, twinkling diamonds loping from your
droopy ears, never to hear the lamenting whimpering whine of the icy
    wind:
"A diamond is forever, a diamond is forever..."
yes...indeed it is...especially to those who must travel this cold,
cruel white world without eyes nor limbs.

This goes out to you too you bamboozled tio tacos and uncle toms,
like greedy imbecilic dorky sell-out money skank Michael Jordan, or P.
    Diddly Squat,
displaying how stupid you twats are in your fictional
commercialized venereal disease advocating hip-hop videos.

The day pimp daddy George Herbert Walker Bush died...I envisioned it
    well:
        one world with no prison cells, one world with clean drinking
water wells, one world where generations X, Y, and Z indiscriminately
uprooted the asphalt beneath their weary death dragging feet, and
replaced the sickening frigid concrete jungle heat with agrarian personal
lots more fruitful and beautiful than the fabricated delusional myth
of Camelot, one world without genetically modified food, one world

without famine, one world without humyn cloning, one world absent maximization of lucre greed, one world doing at least one good deed, one world led by an international body that didn't govern, rule, nor convicted, but made damn sure self-determination and inalienable rights were protected against the totalitarian regimes of corporate conglomerate fiends, one world without multi-national corporations, one world with no hierarchy, one world without money, one world with no taste for milk or honey, one world where our leaders did not lead us astray straight towards perdition, our leaders turned out to be teachers, nurses, dishwashers and soft spoken morticians that didn't act like election seeking politicians, but comforted our bequeathed and guided us towards our initial journey to celestial salvation through communal redemption, one world that employed healers instead of lunatic doctors pursuing a profit over the all too important health and well being of those that suffer, one world with one health plan that didn't require a fiscal buffer as a prerequisite to have access to all the cures they already possess, one world without outer space spy satellites, one world without socialites, one world lacking an uncivilized death penalty, one world where a womyn's abortion rights remain immaculate and legal, one world where if a fateful individual's diseased mortality is in fatal jeopardy, than the idiosyncratic choice for euthanasia is regal, one world where our educational system wasn't run by petty power hungry misfits, our children were taught to disobey autocratic authority and allowed to say what they wanted to say, creatively play at least half of the day, to be able to learn and think would cost nothing, our schools were not abused nor used for brainwashing, indoctrination, or social conditioning, one world without mass media and international press without the people's input and consent, one world where the self-proclaimed decent of society were held in contempt, one world without armies, lawyers, rent-a-thugs, mafias, secret police, or judges, one world with no military tribunals setting irreversible strong-arm precedents, parading past president's grudges, one world where guns, bullets, rocket missiles and bombs were the only things destroyed, one world where girls became boys and boys became girls, one world where the old were young and given our utmost attention, one world without aristocratic pretension, one world that didn't furiously promote sex, violence, and death as an easily achievable commodity, one world, one socialist democratic anarchistic free loving responsible community, one world superfluous with kindness, one world without superpowers, one world where we didn't think we had to live by the hour, one world without state terrorism sponsored by federal tax paying idiots, one world without sword mongering religious zealots, one world without temples, churches, mosques, banks, nuclear research centers, nuclear plants, nuclear dumpsites, and nuclear silos, one world where everybody is allowed to mend their fragmented haloes and melting wings from rising too high to fall too low, one world that didn't produce more numismatic slaves and whores, one world that enjoyed contributing to everyone else's chores, one world with no wars, one world where we can all sing without being censored, one world where we can intellectually moan with no retaliation, dissent without hostile confrontation, one world, one world, no more nations.

The day George Herbert Walker Bush died....
George W. Bush was ultimately, insignificantly assassinated
like a rising star within right-wing European Dutch factions...
sometimes violent political direct action
is what you need to rid the world
of the truly evil seed only to become a major player yourself
in the never-ending game of iniquity.
The world is in bad health.
There are no solutions, only revolutionary answers.
Let us not become soporific statistical collateral damage
due to the mind controlling, propagandistic
malignant tumors pirating our independent thoughts.
Turn the T.V., DVD, and blood splattering Video Games off,
read a leftist unconventional independently published book,
or internet website;
not a mainstream newspaper or magazine.
Too many people have died for nothing.
Too many species have become extinct for dominion.
It may take a nation of millions to hold us back Chuck...
humph...maybe that's why I just don't give a fuck.

The day George Herbert Walker Bush died...

I experienced peace on Earth for the first and only last time.
The melodious chime of children's laughter made me hope
there was not a life hereafter.
The day George Herbert Walker Bush died...
I tried to tell myself that everything would be alright,
but I lied.
The day George Herbert Walker Bush died...
I cried.

The Broken Heart

I know what it feels like to be raped.

Yesterday…Laura Bush and her bastard husband
trespassed on sacred land where I grew up and
have lived all my life.

I know what it feels like to be an Arab.

I hate George W. Bush.
I never thought I would be capable of such hate but I hate him.
I do.
I hate his condescending grin, his ideology of sin.
I hate his psychology of depravity, his perverted Christianity,
I hate the son-of-a-bitch, the son-of-a-whore.
I hate him for making me hate him.

Yesterday…the self-appointed president of the Unilateral Satanic
Association trespassed on sacred land that once was my barrio, my
beloved neighborhood.
This was the place where I hesitantly hugged my first girlfriend
that didn't even really like me;
the place where I learned how to put a lopsided basketball through an
iron hoop; El Torreon, Alto St., the original Westside of Santa Fe…
the place where I learned how to love.

I hate him, I really do.

I can recall cautious autumn drizzles,
walking home from Gonzales Elementary
with three or four of my friends on the cracked sidewalks of West
    Alameda St.,
breaking our mother's backs,

throwing rocks the size of an eight ball of cocaine
at passerby automobiles, hoping you were the one
that first landed a strike on top of the tin roof or aluminum hood of an
    arbitrary car
like a misguided ballistic missile loaded with depleted uranium
landing somewhere in some Baghdad supermarket,
far away from here.

West Alameda St.,
el camino mi madre y padre saved from rabid developers
that destroyed the sacred land of this unholy city with no faith.
West Alameda St.,
where my mother and father held my nervous hand
showing me, teaching me what it takes to realistically
organize people around a just cause: just cuz they
wanted to make the world a better place for me and
my brothers to live in.
West Alameda St.,
my mother became Mayor because of this issue;
only to confront ethnocentric diminution from a hostile imperial society,
she and my father defeated City Hall and its hand out corruption.
They were there, they were always there...
distributing petitions, making sure people signed them, making sure
the people understood the nature of their persecution.
They were the only ones at the neighborhood meetings with reason,
spelling out the truth, last ones to speak, riling up the meek,
seeking any path—in out around inside behind the seemingly
    insurmountable system—while the newly infiltrated gringo that
    shared the same concern spoke of
Marxism, Communism, Socialism, Spiritualism, ideas, ideas, ideas but
only speaking of liberal ideas because somehow for some reason the
    gringo
just wasn't willing to commit treason against its system that it benefits
    from.
But my mother and father were there,
West Alameda St.,

doing whatever it took to end the crookedness of the highway
expansion project,
and its suit and tie progenitors.
They taught me that sacrifice is love.

I know what it feels like to be alone.

I remember one incident in particular...forever.
We were at the Ortega house at the bottom of the street we lived
on—this small, square box of an adobe shelter that had been there
longer than it took the white man pioneer to slaughter all the buffalo
in the West. *The Exorcist* was on in black and white and I was scared
out of my eight-year old innocence. Linda Blair was getting ready to
throw-up all over the priest in the hospital room when I turned away
out of fear only to see my mother and father explaining to the entire
Ortega family—especially the viejita matriarch with her children and
grandchildren surrounding her—explaining to them how the city, along
with its business partners of insensitive, money driven developers, were
going to take their home so they could turn the two-lane community
street of West Alameda into a four-lane highway that would transport
more eighteen wheeler semi-trucks, noise, and pollution than the CIA
transports heroin and cocaine into big city urban ghettoes and small
Northern New Mexican villages. I saw how after my parents were
through explaining the issue, educating, there was not one member
of the Ortega family that was not infuriated, especially the viejita. The
injustice had registered. Now, today when I turn off West Alameda St.
onto my beloved Bob St., the first thing I see is this huge monstrosity of
an Amerikan flag flying outside on the porch of the Ortega house, ever
since the bombing began in Afghanistan, old stars and stripes, swaying
like a sultry siren in a swarthy tavern teasing me, mocking me, laughing
in my embarrassed, downtrodden face. Everyday each time I see that
flag I feel like throwing up.

The Chicano, my broken heart...
my brethren of bamboozled bewilderment.
Why is it that every time I attend peace rallies or anti-war
    demonstrations

in Santa I am the only spic in sight? Chicanos, aren't you at least half of the city's population?

Yesterday...it was you Chicano that was driving by on West Alameda St.
throwing fingers, hollering threats, showing thumbs down, hiding your
    brown skin
behind your badge acting all bad calling us a bunch of fags because we
    do not support
this militaristic sickness that is the Amerikan Empire.
The Chicano, my broken heart...
it should be you out here,
it is your children dying and murdering for Bush and his billionaire
    business partners
it is your children locked-up in some prison cell somewhere in
    disproportionate numbers
it is your children on death row in Texas
it is your children knocked-up at fifteen
it is your children shooting each other in East L.A, Albuquerque, and
    Santa Fe
it is your children harassed by police
it is your children given no opportunity
             no immunity
          no peace.
Chicano, my broken heart...
when will you start to realize that you are a conquered people?
Robbed of land, water, and dignity
robbed of religion, family, and community.
Chicano of Santa Fe, the gringo needs you;
he needs your warrior spirit because he is a coward.
These liberal progressive fools do nothing except play by the rules,
and what's worse is they feel good about themselves when it's over.

I know what it feels like to be alone.

Yesterday...my roots were ripped from the soil,
my memories forgotten, my childhood molested.
Yesterday...Laura Bush and her scumbag husband
invaded my privacy, my consecrated sanctuary.

I couldn't stop crying.
The wind was wicked, blowing dust particles in my squinting eyes. I felt
she was trying to blind me, preventing me from witnessing the
     disgusting
display that was taking place.
Karma and her legion of angelic spirits were furious.
An ominous presence of magnanimous evil overcame me
the minute he set foot in Santa Fe at the airport.
How could you let this little prick come into your neighborhood, *your*
     neighborhood? where you learned how to ride a bike,
where you learned how to drive a car,
where you lost your virginity,
where you were almost kidnapped,
where you met your first friend that later on in life at the age of nineteen
     hanged himself on the goal posts of the Alameda Junior High
     football field, in your neighborhood,
your neighborhood, Alto St.—Alto Park—
how could you allow this filth to defecate on the grass
where you engaged in countless shaving cream fights,
where you traveled throughout the city sewer tunnels for miles,
where you first inhaled marijuana,
where you played little league baseball,
where you swung on swings,
where you felt the subtlety of guitar strings,
where you played catch with your father,
where you walked your dogs wrestling for fun,
where you built snow people and threw snowballs,
where you lived life like it should be lived by everyone,
especially when they are young.
How could you allow this to happen?

Yesterday…Secret service in the service of secret armies and shadow
     governments
drove by in the passenger seats of the patrolling pigs
down West Alameda St, in front of Bob St.,
diggin my Che Guevara shirt, registering through their scheming eyelids
     behind

secret agent shades, my scornful, concerned, frustrated countenance,
tousled hippie azulejo hair and insurrectionary gestures; they were
    saying
I was a potential troublemaker.
If they only knew...
If they only knew how I have given up.
If they only knew how disconcerted I was with the whole peace so-
    called movement in Santa Fe. If only they could feel how worthless
    and ineffectual it all is.
If only they could see how disappointing it is to see hundreds of people
    come together only to depart when they are told, only to stay
    put where they are told, only to come together once more if the
    appropriate permit for protest is bequeathed.
Permit for protest...PERMIT FOR PROTEST...
I'm enslaved by bewilderment.
I am so disheartened.
I am so disgusted with the hypocritical play it safe liberals and
    progressives.
That is why I designate myself as a far left anarchist radical Chicano.
That is why I am nothing.

I know what it feels like to be defeated.

I hate Amerika.
Yes. I am anti-Amerikan.
There will never be peace for any human being until Amerika is no
    longer an empire,
                                        no longer an entity.
Amerika is hate,
Amerika is greed.
Amerika is a selfish, overweight nation jacked-up on manufactured
    speed known as underpaid hand picked caffeine. Amerika is oil.
    Amerika is blood, sweat, and toil. Amerika is death. Amerika is far
    too spoiled. Amerika is your HMO. Amerika is reaping what it has
    sowed. Amerika is unhealthy, that's because it's way too wealthy.
    Amerika is pollution. Amerika is not the solution, but capitalistic
    prostitution. Amerika is institutionalization. Amerika is alcoholism

and substance abuse. Amerika does not reduce its use. Amerika is sponsorship of Third World dictatorship. Amerika is censorship. Amerika has declared war on all forms of art, on the working class. Amerika is a stinky, slimy fart…the gas that just passed from my ass to the toxic air. No one in Amerika cares. Amerika puts guns in the hands of children and encourages them to kill. Amerika needs to chill. Amerika is the ever-present, ever-growing prescription pill you can't afford. Amerika is bored. Amerika is the biggest whore. Amerika is corporate controlled. Amerika is on a roll to becoming the best fascist state of all time. Amerika is a war crime. Everyone in Amerika is just doing time. Amerika is a flourishing prison industry. Amerika is not the land of the free. Amerika is stupidity plus conformity equals slavery. Amerika is nuclear energy. Amerika is the enormity of aggressive unsympathetic egos. Amerika is pathetic. Amerika is me first, you last. Amerika keeps the rest of the world living in a permanent cast. Amerika is hypocrisy. Amerika's only philosophy is maximization of profit. Amerika is elitism. Amerika is racism. Amerika is imperialism, colonialism. Amerika is corrupt. Amerika is devastation, self-destruction. Amerika anymore just doesn't function. Amerika is silent. Amerika is way too violent. Amerika is anti-intellectual. Amerika has too many contrary ideas about being sexual. Amerika is syphilis, gonorrhea, chlamydia, HIV, herpes. Amerika is a disease. Amerika is a theocracy. Amerika is the non-debated Amerikan police state. No matter what anyone says, Amerika is not great. Amerika is fake. Amerika is one big lie agreed upon. Amerika is wrong. Amerika is misbehaving. Amerika is dying and it is not worth saving…

It was founded on slaughter, it lives through slaughter, and it will perish in slaughter.
Teach your sons and daughters the truth,
or you too may become victims to the next generation of out-of-control spoiled youth.

Yesterday…Amerika came to my vulnerable heart and tore it apart.
Now I can see—whatever happens in Washington D.C. *does* affect me.
Laura Bush and her bird-witted husband traveled throughout my

neighborhood
without any kind of disruption. Alto St., Alto Park, El Torreon, the
    aboriginal
Westside of Santa Fe...and all I did was turn away.
This used to be the neighborhood with a bad reputation,
the place you respected otherwise get ejected.
Now it's just another gentrified section of the city, housing liberal
    windbags.
Too bad,
Yesterday...at least one person should have been arrested.

I know what it feels like to be defeated.

Yesterday...I was raped.
I was shivering, shaking, lamenting, confused and depressed.
I felt so ashamed I thought I was the one to blame.
I take no pride in my Spanish surname.
From an Indio and a Moore my heritage remains.
They came...They...yesterday...the infamous They.
The ones ruining everything—the Earth, the world, humanity, my life.
They...the ones creating, continuously generating all the strife.
Alto St., El Torreon, the original Westside of Santa Fe,
West Alameda St., Alto Park...Alto Park:
the place I grew-up and have lived and have lost.

One time there was this homeless person sleeping in one of the little
league baseball dugouts. This was before the police started cracking
down on this activity and started throwing them in jail. This was before
the Gringo took over my neighborhood. It was almost nighttime in
the middle of autumn and the winds were starting to increase. The
temperature was dropping. I was walking home from a friend's house
when I saw this ragged man, looked something like a tecato, passed out
on the bench inside one of the dugouts. I recognized him. I used to see
him there all the time. His bottle of Mad Dog was empty lying on the
concrete floor underneath his dangling arm right next to his trash bags
filled with clothes and other personal items. He was snoring. Raindrops
slightly began to fall. I stared at this man for a while wondering if he

had any family, wondering if he had any place to go. I thought of all the times I had sat right where he was sleeping and smelled urine. I wondered if maybe he was the dude that would piss all over the dugouts. It didn't matter. Visions of jubilation, excitement, and frivolity attacked my consciousness. Visions of innocence. As the rain soaked my uncombed hair dripping from the tip of my nose, I thought about how many times that same dugout provided asylum for me from the cruelty and mean spiritedness stemming from coaches, teammates, and parents all participating in the vicious orgy of competitive sports. I thought about all the times I used to prefer to just stay in the dugout throughout the course of a baseball game instead of going out onto the field, afraid of making a mistake and have to endure the punishment of ridicule and harassment. I figured if that dugout could provide shelter and protection for me, then it certainly was good enough to provide the same for that anonymous gentleman. So I ran home, ran back and placed a wool blanket over his body and left five dollars for him in his coat pocket. I never saw him again.

Alto Park—the place where I learned how to love.

Yesterday…Alto Park:
In Junior High, attending Alameda Junior High School, I witnessed this fight at Alto Park between two eighth grade girls. There was a big crowd. Most of them were cheering on this one girl named Melissa. She was the favorite. I don't know why they were fighting, nobody ever does. Fights used to be pretty common at Alto Park. Anyhow, before the fight commenced I noticed that Melissa's opponent had very few people supporting her and looked awfully timid and apprehensive. She was much smaller than Melissa. I felt sorry for her. She had an exquisite calm demeanor on her expression. Melissa ambushed her. Shortly after the brawl began, the crowd closed in on the two as they wrestled on the grass pulling hair, scratching, choking, and biting. Suddenly, like a surprise explosion, the crowd backed off, opened up and I saw Melissa's forehead covered in bright red blood, trickling down from her scalp. Apparently the other girl had pulled out a pair of brass knuckles and clocked Melissa on the head opening a gash that wouldn't stop bleeding. The fight didn't end there. Melissa jumped to her feet, chasing

the other girl all over the park, through the river, throwing rocks and sticks at her all the while with blood pouring over her face and neck. She never did catch up with her. That was the first time I had ever seen blood appear in a fight. An overwhelming shutter of trepidation apprehended me and I felt like running away, but I stayed put, frozen, terrified that the people watching might take me for a punk. I was so scared I didn't know what to do. I didn't know how to absorb such violence, certain I would never embrace it.

I know what it feels like to be afraid.

Yesterday…I was violated.
The land I love, the neighborhood I breathe, the city I sense was scarred.
I hate George W. Bush and his mother of a wife Laura.
I hate them, I really do.
I hate them for making me hate them,
I hate myself for indulging in such hate.
I don't want to feel like this anymore.
I don't know what to do.
Obviously the peace demonstrations in Santa Fe are lame and
achieve nothing but self-righteous platitude.
I do not agree entirely with the non-violent attitude, yet…I still don't
    know what to do.
Sometimes I fantasize and try to convince myself that if Bush were to be
    assassinated
or if his daughters were to be kidnapped, or his father murdered,
or any conservative republican billionaire statesman or businessman
    were to be killed,
I would feel alright.
I think of all the ignorant stupid fanatical sheep out there waving their
    flags, repeating what they hear on television and how I would love
    nothing more than to punch them in their ridiculous face or put a
    bullet in their head,
and that this would make me feel better…
but it's just not true…it's just not true…
I just don't know what to do.

My mother recently told me:

"Those willing to stand up and fight, throwing stones at tanks, have
conviction. They believe in the goodness...the beauty of struggle."

The Gringo has no conviction, the Chicano is an idiot that doesn't
    believe.

I may never be ready to kill for what I believe in,
but I am prepared to die for my convictions.

Printed in the United States
143060LV00003B/23/A

9 780865 346251